Answers

Answers

Discussions with Western Buddhists

by

The Dalai Lama

edited by

José Ignacio Cabezón

Snow Lion Publications
Ithaca, New York

Snow Lion Publications
P.O. Box 6483
Ithaca, New York 14851 USA
Tel: 607-273-8519
www.snowlionpub.com

Printed in U.S.A.

ISBN 1-55939-162-6

Library of Congress Cataloging-in-Publication Data
Bstan-'dzin-rgya-mtsho, Dalai Lama XIV, 1935–
    Answers : discussions with Western Buddhists / edited by José
Ignacio Cabezón.
        p. cm.
Rev. ed. of: The Bodhgaya interviews, 1988.
    ISBN 1-55939-162-6 (alk. paper)
1. Buddhism—Doctrines—Miscellanea.
2. Buddhism—China—Tibet—Doctrines—Miscellanea.
3. Bstan-'dzin-rgya-mtsho, Dalai Lama XIV, 1935– —Interviews.
4. Dalai lamas—Interviews. I. Cabezón, José Ignacio, 1956–
II. Bstan-'dzin-rgya-mtsho, Dalai Lama XIV, 1935– Bodhgaya interviews.
    BQ7935.B774 B55 2001
    294.3'923--dc21
                                                    2001003487

Table of Contents

Editor's Introduction

Of all the sites sacred to Buddhists, Bodhgaya is perhaps the most important. Little more than a village on the outskirts of Gaya, one of the larger cities in the state of Bihar (North India), it has nonetheless attracted Buddhist pilgrims for centuries. Over the past several years, it has become a well established tradition for His Holiness the Dalai Lama to spend several days in January or February in residence in Bodhgaya. During this time, Buddhists from all over the world gather to listen to the teachings of His Holiness and to share in days of prayer and meditation. Especially for the Tibetan Buddhists in exile, for the thousands who flock from Tibet for this occasion, and for the Indian Buddhists from the border areas of Ladakh, Kunu, Arunachal Pradesh and so forth, it is an opportunity not only to make pilgrimage to the place of the Buddha's enlightenment, to pray and to make prostrations under the Bodhi tree, and to circumambulate the central temple, it is an opportunity to engage in all of these practices during the visit of the Dalai Lama, who for them and for thousands of other Buddhists throughout the world, is a source of inspiration and the embodiment of living and active Buddhist principles.

For the community of Western Buddhists as well, winter in Bodhgaya is a time for rejoicing, meeting old friends, and especially for practicing mental cultivation. Several meditation courses meet during this time, and there is usually some form of translation available for those who wish to attend the teachings of His Holiness. In addition, beginning in 1981, His Holiness has given group interviews to the Westerners.

Sometimes the discussions, which invariably have taken the form of question and answer sessions, were granted to groups at the close of a meditation retreat and were restricted to those who participated in that retreat (as in the case with the second discussion in this collection). The majority of the meetings, however, were open to the general public. They were held, almost exclusively, in the Tibetan Temple in Bodhgaya.

Because of the spontaneous and dialogical nature of the interviews, they tended to differ in mood and content from year to year. Still, they all share one common quality: that the questions asked are topical, the issues dealt with reflecting the current concerns of the participants, both Buddhist and non-Buddhist. In a very real way, the questions raised bring up problems that all of us face today. The range of topics is vast. We find philosophical discussions of the doctrine of emptiness, questions concerning the role of monks and nuns in the world today, and debates concerning particle physics, not to speak of questions dealing with politics, psychology, and Tantra. In short, within these few pages, we find the entire gamut of religious and secular human concerns.

I myself was present at the first discussion and was the translator for the fourth. I have witnessed through the years the uniqueness of these occasions, and so, when I was approached to bring out that year's discussion in published form, I realized how worthwhile it would be to compile the Bodhgaya discussions in a single volume. To this end, I have gone through tapes of all of the discussions, have scrutinized all portions in which His Holiness spoke in Tibetan to insure accuracy and to avoid the types of omissions to which spontaneous translation is heir. I have, of course, edited the entire text. Nonetheless, with a view to preserving the original flavor of the dialogues as much as possible, I have tried to keep editing to a minimum.

Thanks must go, first and foremost, to His Holiness the Dalai Lama for giving us the opportunity to present our questions and concerns to him in a way which so easily facilitated discussion. Thanks must also go to Dr. Alex Berzin and Professor Jeffrey Hopkins, who also acted as translators during the discussions. I must also thank Miss Joyce Murdoch, who greatly facilitated my task by so kindly presenting me with the copies of taped discussions in her possession. Finally, the Venerable Thubten Pemo and Miss Sheila Kim were of immense help in typing initial drafts of the text.

It is my hope that this short work will bring to the reader a flavor of winter days in Bodhgaya, a very special time in a very special place — a time of days spent in the warm sun listening to the words of His Holiness and of nights spent in the brilliance of the thousands of candles that devout Buddhists offer at the main temple. Truly, there is no greater nostalgia than for times of holiness.

May this work help to break down the barriers separating human beings from each other. May it increase compassion and insight throughout the world.

José Ignacio Cabezón

The First Discussion

Welcome, I am very glad to meet with you all here. I am open to your questions.

Question: **Do you see any possibility of an integration of Christianity and Buddhism in the West? An overall religion for Western society?**

His Holiness: It depends upon what you mean by integration. If you mean by this the possibility of the integration of Buddhism and Christianity within a society, where they co-exist side by side, then I would answer affirmatively. If, however, your view of integration envisions all of society following some sort of composite religion which is neither pure Buddhism nor pure Christianity, then I would have to consider this form of integration implausible.

It is, of course, quite possible for a country to be predominantly Christian, and yet some of the people of that country

11

choose to follow Buddhism. I think it is quite possible that a person who is basically Christian, who accepts the idea of a God, who believes in God, could at the same time incorporate certain Buddhist ideas and techniques into his or her practice. The teachings of love, compassion, and kindness are present in Christianity as well as in Buddhism. Particularly in the Bodhisattva vehicle, there are many techniques which focus on developing compassion, kindness, etc. There are things which can be practiced at the same time by Christians and Buddhists. While remaining committed to Christianity, it is quite conceivable that a person may choose to undergo training in meditation, concentration, and one-pointedness of mind, or that, while remaining a Christian, one may choose to practice Buddhist ideas. This is another possible and very viable kind of integration.

Question: **Is there any conflict between the Buddhist teachings and the idea of a creator-god who exists independently from us?**

His Holiness: If we view the world's religions from the widest possible viewpoint and examine their ultimate goal, we find that all of the major world religions, whether Christianity or Islam, Hinduism or Buddhism, are dedicated to the achievement of permanent human happiness. They are all directed toward that goal. All religions emphasize the fact that the true follower must be honest and gentle, in other words, that a truly religious person must always strive to be a better human being. To this end, the different world religions teach different doctrines which will help transform the person. In this regard, all religions are the same, there is no conflict. This is something we must emphasize. We must consider the question of religious diversity from this viewpoint. And when we do, we find no conflict.

Now from the philosophical point of view, the theory that God is the creator, is almighty, and permanent is in contradiction to the Buddhist teachings. From this point of view there is disagreement. For Buddhists, the universe has no first cause and hence no creator, nor can there be such a thing as a permanent, primordially pure being. So, of course, doctrinally, there is a conflict. The views oppose one another. But if we consider the purpose of these very different philosophies, then we see that they are the same. This is my belief.

Different kinds of food have different tastes: one may be very hot, one may be very sour, and one very sweet. They are opposite tastes, they conflict. But whether a dish is concocted to taste sweet, sour, or hot, it is nonetheless made in this way so as to taste good. Some people prefer very spicy, hot foods with a lot of chili peppers. Many Indians and Tibetans have a liking for such dishes. Others are very fond of bland tasting foods. It is a wonderful thing to have variety. It is an expression of individuality; it is a personal thing.

Likewise, the variety of the different world religious philosophies is a very useful and beautiful thing. For certain people, the idea of God as creator and of everything depending on His will is beneficial and soothing, and so for that person such a doctrine is worthwhile. For someone else, the idea that there is no creator, that ultimately one is oneself the creator — in that everything depends upon oneself — is more appropriate. For certain people, it may be a more effective method of spiritual growth, it may be more beneficial. For such persons, this idea is better, and for the other type of person, the other idea is more suitable. You see, there is no conflict, no problem. This is my belief.

Now, conflicting doctrines are something which is not unknown even within Buddhism itself. The Mādhyamikas and Cittamatrins, two Buddhist philosophical sub-schools, accept the theory of emptiness. The Vaibhāṣikas and Sautrāntikas, two others, accept another theory, the theory of selflessness, which, strictly speaking, is not the same as the doctrine of emptiness posited by the two higher schools. So there exists this difference, some schools accepting the emptiness of phenomena and others not. There also exists a difference in the way that the two upper schools explain the doctrine of emptiness. For the Cittamatrins, emptiness is set forth in terms of the non-duality of subject and object. The Mādhyamikas, however, repudiate the notion that emptiness is tantamount to idealism, the claim that everything is of the nature of mind. So you see, even within Buddhism, the Mādhyamikas are again divided into Prāsaṅgikas and Svātantrikas, and between these two sub-schools there is also conflict. The latter accepts that things exist by virtue of an inherent characteristic, while the former does not.

So you see, conflict in the philosophical field is nothing to be surprised at. It exists even within Buddhism itself.

Question: **Could you explain what is meant by inherent existence and what the different views are in regard to this? Mādhyamikas (Prāsaṅgikas) claim that there is no inherent existence, whereas other Buddhist schools say there is. Could you discuss these controversies and explain how we can penetrate or see through this illusion of inherent existence?**

His Holiness: In general, the term "inherent existence" has different connotations. Sometimes it is used to refer to the nature of things. For example, we say that "heat" is the nature of fire and that "liquidity and fluidity" are the nature of water. When we use the words "inherent existence" in this way, i.e. as synonymous with "nature," we are using them to refer to things which *do* exist. But there is a form of inherent existence which does not exist, and this is what is criticized in the Mādhyamika analysis. It is the notion that things exist in and of themselves without depending upon other things. In particular, the inherent existence that is the focus of the Mādhyamika critique is a form of existence which does not depend upon conceptual labeling, where the thing labeled does not depend upon conceptual thought for its existence and instead exists by virtue of some nature, or essence, which is inherent within it. Now, except for the Prāsaṅgikas, all other Buddhist schools assert that phenomena are not merely labeled by conceptual thought but, on the contrary, that there is to be found within the object itself something which is the object, i.e. an exemplification of the object. This is what it means to accept inherent existence. The Prāsaṅgikas, however, assert that phenomena exist merely as entities labeled by conceptual thought — that there is nothing to be found within the object which *is* the object itself.

How then does this mistaken idea, that things exist from their own side, operate? Whatever appears to the mind appears as if it existed truly from its own side. For instance, when you look at me, at the Dalai Lama, I appear as though I were something that existed independently and from its own side. The Dalai Lama who is sitting on the cushion does not at all appear as if he were merely labeled by conceptual thought, does he? He appears as though he were not an entity merely labeled by conceptual thought, but instead, as if he existed within the object itself. Now if the object existed as it appears to you, then, when you searched for it, you could actually find a real Dalai Lama. So, we must ask ourselves whether or not this object, when searched for, is to be found or not. If the object is not found when it is searched for, we must conclude that it does not exist from its own side, that when the label is applied to its basis, it is not so labeled because the basis somehow bears within it something which is the object. At this point, one must conclude that the object does not exist as it appears to, but then, one may wonder whether it exists at all.

Things, however, are not utterly non-existent. They *do* exist nominally. So things do exist, but they do not exist from the side of the basis of the label. And hence, though they do exist, because they do not exist within the object itself, they must exist only as they are labeled by the subject (the conceptual mind, for example). There is no other way for the object to exist apart from the way it is posited by conceptual thought. This is then what we mean when we say that all phenomena are merely labeled by conceptual thought. However, things do not appear to us as if they were mere conceptually labeled entities. Instead, they appear as if they existed from their own side. Therefore, it is a mistake to think that things exist as they appear.

There is a difference between the kind of mistake involved in things merely passively appearing to one in this false way and in one's actively asserting through logical argumentation that things must exist in this false way. The difference between these two forms of ignorance, one passive and innate and one active and philosophical in nature, is something that we can gradually come to understand. There exists a difference between the way things exist and the way they appear. Because things appear to us in a way that is at odds with the way in which they actually exist, that is different from their true nature, our thoughts are said to be mistaken. We are said to be deceived.

Roughly speaking, the theory goes something like that. This subject, you see, is not an easy one at all. First of all, it requires one to think very deeply, to investigate very profoundly, the nature of phenomena. Secondly, the process of investigation itself requires both analytical and stabilizing forms of meditation. Without analyzing the object, there is no way that one can ascertain it; without the stabilizing form of meditation which focuses the mind single-pointedly upon the object, even if one has ascertained it, one will find it difficult to perceive the object clearly. So, you see, both of these kinds of meditation are necessary. Both the one which analyzes and the one which just concentrates upon the object are essential. In addition, to understand reality, it is a prerequisite to have accumulated merit. When all of these conditions have been fulfilled, then the understanding of emptiness will increase. But the time factor is also important. This is not something that can be rushed.

Question: **Western science has made advances over the years which, in some respects, seem to contradict the Buddha's teachings. For example, Buddhism asserts that space is permanent, while Western scientists now seem to think that space is impermanent. Also, there is the question of partless particles. These, contrary to the tenets of the highest Buddhist schools, are posited by Western scientists today. If one is following the Buddhist path and encounters experimental evidence for the existence of things which** contradicts Buddhist teachings, then which way does one go? Does one, out of faith, accept what the Buddha said despite contradictory evidence?

His Holiness: This is a very good question. In regard to space, I think that perhaps you are mistaken. There are two different things which could conceivably be called space: one is non-composite space (*du ma byed kyi nam mkha'*), the other is atmospheric space (*bar snang*). Non-composite space refers to the absence of touch and obstruction, and this is what is believed to be permanent. What you are calling "space" is, I believe, what we refer to as "atmospheric space" and this is something we *do* accept as impermanent, as changing. What is more, it is said to have color and so forth. So, I think the English word "space" has more the connotation of our Tibetan word *bar snang* in the sense of atmospheric space.

Questioner: According to Einstein's theory of gravitation, it is the actual lack of obstruction which changes. Matter and space can be conceived of as two kinds of the same substance, so that matter affects space, actually affects the non-obstruction. For example, light traveling in space will travel in a straight line, but when it approaches a material object, it travels in a curved path. This is because the matter has affected the actual structure of the space, the actual nature of the non-obstruction. Space could actually transform from non-obstructing to obstructing and vice versa.

His Holiness: So you are saying that space is not mere lack of tangibility and obstruction, and hence what you are referring to is not non-composite space, but atmospheric space. Atmospheric space is a composite entity. That kind of space which you say changes into something which obstructs must be a composite entity and hence must be atmospheric space. Non-composite space is the actual absence, or emptiness, of material substance; it is the absence of obstruction and tangibility; it is the absence of material impediment, a kind of emptiness. I think that this is a terminological problem. Your English word "space," I think refers more to what we call "atmospheric space" and not to "non-composite space."

Now your second question has to do with elementary particles which are partless. It does seem as though modern physics accepts some sort of elementary partless particle. One begins with a physical form that can be seen by the eye and analyzes it, subdividing it further and further experimentally. One finally is said to reach a substantial entity which can no longer be subdivided, and that is said to be partless. As long as it can be further subdivided, it is said to have parts, and when one reaches the limits of divisibility, that entity is said to be partless.

The Buddhist notion of partlessness, or its refutation, is not something that is actually based on experimentation. The Buddhist discussion of this subject does not deal with the empirical division of matter into different parts. It is instead a theoretical treatment of the possibility of spatial, or dimensional, partlessness that we set forth. In regards to consciousness, it is not spatial partlessness that is discussed (since consciousness is non-material and hence non-spatial) but temporal partlessness. So, in discussions of partlessness, the "parts" being referred to in the Buddhist context are not empirically tested distinct subdivisions. Instead, material things are divided into spatial parts, and consciousness is divided into temporal parts in a strictly theoretical and abstract way.

Physicists claim that gross matter is the accumulation of elementary particles, that subatomic particles in various configurations are what constitute gross matter. Now let us consider the case that elementary particles are spatially partless. If a particle cannot be said to have a side that faces the west and another side that faces the east (since according to our original premise it is said to have no spatial parts), then, when, in the process of accumulating to form a mass, one particle comes to touch another, they would merge, and particles could never amass into larger groupings.

Questioner: **That this is the way elementary particles interact or accumulate is not accepted by Western science.**

His Holiness: Then, according to Western science, do these most elementary particles accumulate at all?

Questioner: **Yes, they accumulate through various interactions to form aggregates of gross matter.**

His Holiness: Now when two of these most elementary of particles come together, do they touch or do they not, and if they do touch, when they do so, do they merge into one or do they retain their individual identity?

Questioner: **Because of the nature of the interaction and because of the "uncertainty principle," questions like this are impossible to answer.**

His Holiness: Well, can you say whether or not the size increases? For example, will there be a difference between the size of a single particle and an aggregate of two, of ten, or of one hundred?

Questioner: **There is certainly a difference between the size of one and an aggregate composed of a very large number of particles.**

His Holiness: If there is a difference between a single particle and an aggregate of one hundred, that means that they accumulate by coming into contact with each other while retaining their individual identity. If, when they came into contact, they merged with one another, larger aggregates could never be formed. And if they do not merge when they come into contact with each other, that implies that a particle must have distinct eastern and western borders, and must therefore have spatial dimensions, in contradiction to the original premise that it was spatially partless.

Now actually, we never empirically subdivided these particles in our analysis, did we? They are too subtle, too small, to have subjected them to the kind of gross analysis at our disposal at present. Still, though the analysis cannot be undertaken empirically by us at this very moment, though we cannot implement it by machine, we have nonetheless been able to conduct it theoretically. We have been able to determine that elementary particles have four sides which are distinct, an eastern side, western side, etc. Hence, since it has these spatial parts, it must have size, it cannot be a dimensionless point.

Questioner: **It doesn't follow that just because you have one hundred particles which have amassed to something larger, that one particle must therefore have directions, since, according to modern physics, what holds the particles together is not their touching each other, but something more subtle, the subatomic forces.**

His Holiness: In any case, this is the situation now, in this century. If we wait another twenty years, the physicists may yet have something else to say. Still, it seems to me that if you think about it logically, should particles be spatially dimensionless points, then an aggregate of one thousand such particles could be no larger than just one of them. If, when a second partless particle combines with a first, they merge, then so would the subsequent combination of one hundred or one thousand particles.

Now for your last question. Suppose that something is definitely proven through scientific investigation. That a certain hypothesis is verified or that a certain fact emerges as a result of scientific investigation. And suppose, furthermore, that that fact is incompatible with Buddhist theory. There is no doubt that we must accept the result of scientific research. You see, the general Buddhist position is that we must accept *fact*. Mere speculation devoid of an empirical basis, when such is possible, will not do. We must always accept the fact. So if an hypothesis has been tested and has been found to be one hundred percent sure, then it is a fact and that is what we must accept.

It is because this notion is at the very core of Buddhist thinking that we can say that the Madhyamaka philosophy is superior to the Cittamātra, that the Cittamātra philosophy is superior to the Sautrāntika, and the Sautrāntika to the Vaibhāṣika — this emerges out of this empirical attitude toward the truth. There are many key points of the Cittamātra philosophy which, when analyzed, can be shown to be philosophically untenable. It is because the Cittamātra view cannot withstand the test of reasoning that the Madhyamaka is said to be superior. All of this is grounded in this one attitude of always accepting reality, that which is fact. Were this not the case, it would be impossible to assert that the Prāsaṅgika Madhyamaka viewpoint was the best and most subtle.

As regards the Buddha's word, i.e. the role of scripture, it is true that both the Madhyamaka and the Cittamātra systems have scriptural basis, both are based on the Buddha's words. Yet, we can distinguish the Prāsaṅgika's doctrines as superior to the Cittamātra's because the former accords with reality whereas the latter does not. So, since we must follow what is factual, what is based on reality, we must follow the Prāsaṅgika theory over that of the Cittamātra. This is the way we must think, it is the general Buddhist attitude. Buddhists believe in rebirth. But suppose that through various investigative means, science one day comes to the definite conclusion that there is no rebirth. If this is definitively proven, then we must accept it and we *will* accept it. This is the general Buddhist idea. So it seems that the scientific method is more powerful! But of course we know that there is a limit to this method also. Let me give you another example. The *Abhidharmakośa* says that the world is flat. But we can all see, we can empirically determine, that the world is round, and so we must accept it as round. We must not require that, despite scientific findings, Buddhists accept the world to be flat simply because it is stated in the *Abhidharmakośa*. That is wrong, and it should not be advocated. But I think that, concerning space, there is no real problem, only a difference in terminology.

Question: **I would like to know the role that consciousness plays in the process of reincarnation.**

His Holiness: In general, there are different levels of consciousness. The more rough, or gross, levels of consciousness are very heavily dependent upon the physical, or material, sphere. Since one's own physical aggregate (the body) changes from birth to birth, so too do these gross levels of consciousness. The more subtle the level of consciousness, however, the more independent of the physical sphere and hence the more likely that it will remain from one life to the next. But in general, whether more subtle or more gross, all levels of consciousness are of the same nature.

Question: **It is generally said that teachers of other religions, no matter how great, cannot attain liberation without turning to the Buddhist path. Now suppose there is a great teacher, say he is a Śaivite, and suppose he upholds very strict discipline and is totally dedicated to other people all of the time, always giving himself. Is this person, simply because he follows Śiva, incapable of attaining liberation, and if so, what can be done to help him?**

His Holiness: During the Buddha's own time, there were many non-Buddhist teachers whom the Buddha could not help, for whom he could do nothing. So he just let them be.

The Buddha Śākyamuni was an extraordinary being, he was the manifestation, the *nirmāṇakāya*, or physical appearance, of an already enlightened being. But while some people recognized him as a Buddha, other regarded him as a black magician with strange and evil powers. So, you see, even the Buddha Śākyamuni himself was not accepted as an enlightened being by all of his contemporaries. Different human beings have different mental predispositions, and there are

cases when even Buddha himself could not do much to overcome these — there was a limit.

Now today, the followers of Śiva have their own religious
practices, and they reap some benefit from engaging in their
own forms of worship. Through this, their life will gradually
change. Now my own position on this question is that Śiva-
ji's followers should practice according to their own beliefs
and traditions, Christians must genuinely and sincerely follow what they believe, and so forth. That is sufficient.

Questioner: **But they will not attain liberation.**

His Holiness: We Buddhists ourselves will not be liberated at
once. In our own case, it will take time. Gradually, we will be
able to reach *mokṣa,* or nirvāṇa, but the majority of Buddhists will not achieve this within their own lifetimes. So
there's no hurry. If Buddhists themselves have to wait, perhaps many lifetimes, for their goal, why should we expect
that it be different for non-Buddhists? So, you see, nothing
much can be done.

Suppose, for example, you try to convert someone from
another religion to the Buddhist religion, and you argue with
them trying to convince them of the inferiority of their position. And suppose you do not succeed, suppose they do not
become Buddhist. On the one hand, you have failed in your
task, and on the other hand, you may have weakened the
trust they have in their own religion, so that they may come
to doubt their own faith. What have you accomplished by

all this? It is of no use. When we come into contact with the followers of different religions, we should not argue. Instead, we should advise them to follow their own beliefs as sincerely and as truthfully as possible. For if they do so, they will no doubt reap certain benefits. Of this there is no doubt. Even in the immediate future, they will be able to achieve more happiness and more satisfaction. Do you agree?

This is the way I usually act in such matters, it is my belief. When I meet the followers of different religions, I always praise them, for it is enough, it is sufficient, that they are following the moral teachings that are emphasized in every religion. It is enough, as I mentioned earlier, that they are trying to become better human beings. This in itself is very good and worthy of praise.

Questioner: **But is it only the Buddha who can be the ultimate source of refuge?**

His Holiness: Here, you see, it is necessary to examine what is meant by liberation or salvation. Liberation in which "a mind that understands the sphere of reality annihilates all defilements in the sphere of reality" is a state that only Buddhists can accomplish. This kind of mokṣa, or nirvāṇa, is only explained in the Buddhist scriptures and is achieved only through Buddhist practice. According to certain religions, however, salvation is a place, a beautiful paradise, like a peaceful valley. To attain such a state as this, to achieve such a state of mokṣa, does not require the practice of emptiness, the understanding of reality. In Buddhism itself, we believe that through the accumulation of merit one can obtain rebirth in heavenly paradises like Tushita.

Questioner: So, if one is a follower of Vedānta, and one reaches the state of *satcitānanda*, would this not be considered ultimate liberation?

His Holiness: Again, it depends upon how you interpret the words "ultimate liberation." The mokṣa which is described in the Buddhist religion is achieved only through the practice of emptiness. And this kind of nirvāṇa, or liberation, as I have defined it above, cannot be achieved even by Svātantrika Mādhyamikas, by Cittamātras, Sautrāntikas, or Vaibhāṣikas. The followers of these schools, though Buddhists, do not understand the actual doctrine of emptiness. Because they cannot realize emptiness, or reality, they cannot accomplish the kind of liberation I defined previously.

Question: Can you explain how Tantric meditation achieves the enlightened state so much more quickly than vipaśyanā, i.e. insight meditation?

His Holiness: In Tantric meditation, particularly in the practice of Anuttarayoga Tantra, while one is realizing emptiness, the ultimate truth, one controls thought through the use of certain techniques. In the Sūtrayāna, the non-Tantric form of the Mahāyāna, there is no mention of these unique techniques involving the yogic practices of controlled breathing and meditation using the inner channels and cakras, etc. The Sūtrayāna just describes how to analyze the object, i.e. how to come to gain insight into the nature of the object through reasoning, etc. The Anuttarayoga Tantra, however, teaches, in addition to this, certain techniques which use the channels, subtle winds, etc. to help one to control one's thoughts more effectively. These methods help one to more quickly gain control over the scattered mind and to achieve more effectively a level of consciousness which is at once subtle and powerful. This is the basis of the system.

The wisdom that realizes emptiness, that has gained insight into the nature of reality, is of varying kinds, depending upon the level of subtlety of the consciousness perceiving the emptiness. In general, there are rough levels of consciousness, more subtle levels, and then the innermost subtle level of consciousness. It is the uncommon characteristic of Tantric practice that through it one can evoke this most subtle consciousness at will and put it to use in a most effective way. For example, when emptiness is realized by this subtlest level of mind, it is more powerful, having a much greater effect on the personality.

In order to activate or make use of the more subtle levels of consciousness, it is necessary to block the rougher levels — the rougher or grosser levels must cease. It is through specifically Tantric practices, such as the meditations on the cakras and the channels (*nadīs*), that one can control and temporarily abandon the rougher levels of consciousness. When these become suppressed, the subtler levels of consciousness become active. And it is through the use of the subtlest level of consciousness that the most powerful spiritual realizations can come about. Hence, it is through the Tantric practice involving the most subtle consciousness that the goal of enlightenment can most quickly be realized.

Questioner: **But aren't the objects of Tantric meditation just imaginary things without any reality?**

His Holiness: Certainly, at the outset these objects are just mind-created. In the beginning of the practice the various objects one realizes are simply imaginary. Nonetheless, they serve a special function and each has a specific purpose. Their being imaginary does not deprive them of efficacy.

Question: **How do things exist if they are empty of inherent existence?**

His Holiness: The doctrines of emptiness and selflessness do not imply the non-existence of things. Things *do* exist. When we say that all phenomena are void of self-existence, it does not mean that we are advocating non-existence, that we are repudiating that things exist. Then what is it we are negating? We are negating, or denying, that anything exists *from its own side without depending on other things.* Hence, it is because things depend for their existence upon other causes and conditions that they are said to lack independent self-existence.

To put it another way, if we search for an object, subjecting it to logical analysis, it cannot be found. Whatever the object may be, whether it is mental or physical, whether it is nirvāṇa or Śākyamuni Buddha himself, nothing can ever be found when it is searched for, when it is subjected to logical inquiry.

Now you see, we have this belief in an "I." We say "I am so and so" or "I am a Buddhist." If we investigate the implications of this, we cannot but conclude that the self, or "I," exists. Where there is a belief, there must be a believer, so there must be sentient beings. There is no question whether or not there exist beings — *of course* beings exist. The Dalai Lama exists. Tibetans exist. There are Canadians and there are the English. Since England exists, there must be Englishmen, and an English language. This is what we are speaking now. That there are beings who are at present speaking English is a fact which no one can deny.

But if we now ask ourselves "where is this English which we are all speaking?," "where are the Englishmen?," "where is the 'I'?," "where is the self of the Dalai Lama?," we might be tempted to say that because no self is to be found when analyzed with logical reasoning, that there is no self *at all*. But this is wrong. We can, for example, point to the Dalai Lama's physical form, his body, and we know that the Dalai Lama has a mind. My body and mind belong to *me*. So if *I* didn't exist at all, then how could I be the "owner" of my body and mind? How could they be "mine"? The body and mind belong to someone, and that someone is the "I." It is because the body belongs to the self that, when we take an aspirin and the body feels better, we say "I feel better." So it is because it is meaningful to say "I am not well" when the body is not well, it is because we sometimes get angry with our*selves* when our mind forgets something and we say, "Oh, I'm so absent-minded," it is because all of these situations and forms of expression do occur and are meaningful, that we know there must exist a conventional, or nominal, "I."

Now, apart from the body and mind, there can be no "I," and yet, if we search for the self among our mental and physical aggregates, there is no "I" to be found. So the point is this: there is an "I" but it is something that is *merely labeled in dependence upon the body and mind.* Now the body itself is something which is material, and it is an entity composed of many parts, and it too, if searched for among those parts, cannot be found.

This applies equally to *all* phenomena, even to Maitreya Buddha himself. If we look for Maitreya Buddha among his aggregates, we cannot find even him. Since ultimately even Buddhas do not exist, we know that ultimately there can be no person, or self, of any kind. However, conventionally, there is a Maitreya Buddha. His statue or image we can see for ourselves here in the temple. Now again, let us consider the image. It has different parts: the head, the torso, the hands, and feet. Apart from these there is no image of Maitreya Buddha. The image is simply a composite of these different parts labeled by the name "image of Maitreya Buddha." So the conclusion is this: if we investigate and search for any object, we could spend years and years and never find it. This means that the image of Maitreya, for example, does not exist from its own side. It is something that is only labeled by our minds. It does not exist inherently, and so it must be an entity only imputed, or labeled, by the mind. Though the image does not ultimately exist, nonetheless, if we take the image as our object in visualization, for example, and worship it, etc., the merit *is* accrued and benefit *will* come.

Questioner: **Then doesn't it follow that the image has the inherent power within it to generate merit for the worshipper?**

His Holiness: Certainly the image has the ability to serve as a basis for the generation of merit. Our having determined that the image is empty of inherent existence does not negate the image's ability to serve as a source or field for the accumulation of merit. But we must keep in mind that the accumulation of merit or of negativity is something that occurs only nominally or conventionally and not ultimately or inherently.

If the image had the *inherent* power to create merit, then it should be able to do so independently of any other factors or conditions, but we know this is not the case. For example, a person who, motivated by hatred, destroys an image does not accumulate virtue from his action in regard to the object, but non-virtue. Those who do prostrations or make offerings to an image without the proper motivation accrue very little merit, while those who perform worship with proper mindfulness and good intentions will benefit greatly from their actions. So, you see, whether or not merit is accrued in regard to the image is not something predetermined and inherent within the image, but something which depends upon other conditions and factors. For this reason, it is said to be a process which exists only conventionally, or nominally.

But faith itself is something which is only mentally labeled. It does not inherently exist. If one analyzes or examines the object labeled by the word "faith," if one searches for it, it cannot be found. But outside of such an examination there does exist such a thing as faith. Faith does *conventionally* exist, for it exists when it is not subjected to analysis. The same is true of blessings: when subjected to logical analysis, they cannot be found, but if one is content not to examine their ultimate mode of existence, then they *can* be said to exist. This is, roughly speaking, the case. Be that as it may, this is a subject that must be given a great deal of thought.

Question: **Could you please give us some brief advice which we can take with us into our daily lives?**

His Holiness: I don't know, I don't really have that much to say. I'll simply say this. We are all human beings, and from this point of view, we are the same. We all want happiness and we do not want suffering. If we consider this point, we will find that there are no differences between people of different faiths, races, colors, or cultures. We all have this common wish for happiness.

Actually, we Buddhists are supposed to save *all* sentient beings, but practically speaking, this may be too broad a notion for most people. In any case, we must at least think in terms of helping all *human* beings. This is very important. Even if we cannot think in terms of sentient beings inhabiting different worlds, we should nonetheless think in terms of the human beings on our own planet. To do this is to take a practical approach to the problem. It is necessary to help others, not only in our prayers, but in our daily lives. If we find we cannot help another, the least we can do is to desist from harming them. We must not cheat others or lie to them. We must be honest human beings, sincere human beings.

On a very practical level, such attitudes are things which we need. Whether one is a believer, a religious person, or not, is another matter. Simply as an inhabitant of the world, as a member of the human family, we need this kind of attitude. It is through such an attitude that real and lasting world peace and harmony can be achieved. Through harmony, friendship, and respecting one another, we can solve many problems in the *right* way, without difficulties.

This is what I believe, and wherever I go, whether it be to a communist country, like the former Soviet Union, or to a capitalist and democratic country like the United States and the countries of Western Europe, I express the same message. This is my advice, my suggestion. It is what I feel. I myself practice this as much as I can. If you find you agree with me and you find some value in what I have said, then it has been worthwhile.

You see, sometimes religious persons, people who are genuinely engaged in the practice of religion, withdraw from the sphere of human activity. In my opinion, this is not good. It is not right. But I should qualify this. In certain cases, when a person genuinely wishes to engage in intense meditation, for example, when someone wishes to attain *śamatha*, then it is all right to seek isolation for certain limited periods of time. But such cases are by far the exception, and the vast majority of us must work out a genuine religious practice within the context of human society.

In Buddhism, both learning and practice are extremely important, and they must go hand in hand. Without knowledge, just to rely on faith, faith, and more faith is good but not sufficient. So the intellectual part must definitely be present. At the same time, strictly intellectual development without faith and practice, is also of no use. It is necessary to combine knowledge born from study with sincere practice in our daily lives. These two must go together.

Let me add just one more thing. We should be in no hurry to practice Tantra. I myself have received many initiations, but it is very difficult to practice Tantra in the right way. So why hurry? Once you are qualified, and have the proper foundation, then one can practice Tantra in the correct way and develop very quickly just as the Tantric scriptures themselves state. But without the proper foundation and without having accumulated the proper conditions, there is no hope to speedily advance in the path through Tantric practice. If one *does* engage in this practice without having fulfilled the proper preconditions, then there is the danger that misconceptions, in the form of doubt, may arise. We see that the texts say that something can be achieved in three months or six months, etc., and when such time has elapsed and nothing has happened, we may begin to wonder whether progress is possible at all, and we begin to have doubts about the method itself. So if we want to practice in a realistic way, we should not be in a hurry to practice Tantra. This is what I feel.

The Second Discussion

First, I would like to say how happy I am about being able to meet you here today. I think this is the second time we have met here, and it seems that this kind of dialogue can be of some help, of some benefit, to people. This is very good. So I am very, very glad to be here once again.

I myself have nothing to say, so I decided to open the floor up for questions since I was wondering what kind of queries you had.

I came with the idea of answering questions, so I came with an interpreter. For the deeper philosophical questions I will need a qualified interpreter. Today I am prepared, and I welcome even the most difficult questions!

Question: **In the past few years and perhaps longer, there has been a growing interest among Westerners, young Westerners primarily, in the spiritual practices and disciplines of Buddhism, and one of the questions that arises for many** people here is: yes, we have the opportunity to practice our meditation, to cultivate through various means our hearts and our minds, but when we go back to the West, the society does not always seem sympathetic.

It becomes a difficulty and a problem living in the Western world. So the question which I would like to ask His Holiness is simply this: What advice does he have for us?

His Holiness: It is true, I agree, the environment is something which is very important. If the environment, the situation one is in, is not so helpful, then even if one *wants* to practice, it is difficult to implement that determination continuously. Here, my advice, my suggestion, is this: if you have some basic knowledge, some basic experience on how to tackle a problem, on how to cope with the kind of unfriendly attitudes that arise in a competitive society, for example, then, once one has created for oneself some kind of foundation, in spite of the fact that one may be living in a society which is not so favorable to the practitioner, it is possible, deep down, to abide by the teachings.

Now, in certain circumstances, it may be necessary to react in different ways. For example, if you are genuinely a humble and honest person and act that way, some people may take advantage of you. So in such a situation, it may be necessary to react. But we should react without bad feelings. Deep down, tolerance, compassion, and patience must still be present, but on a superficial level, we take the appropriate action. This may be the only way to proceed in such a situation.

Another advisable thing is that, from time to time, you come to a place, like Bodhgaya, where you can get teachings and where you have the environment with the proper facilities to practice. From time to time we must recharge, then we can return to our work or to our studies, etc. Instead of spending money on a vacation at a beach resort, for example, we can come to a site such as this and refresh our minds. This, I think, is helpful. It is the middle way, the proper way. That is my feeling.

Question: **If a person views the self and other phenomena as being empty of any inherent existence, is it then, in that state, possible for them to take any animate or inanimate phenomenon as their object, and through the power of imputation or words, enable that object to actually take on a manifesting role with the qualities which we view objects to have?**

His Holiness: This is an instance of not properly understanding the meaning of "lack of inherent existence." If we think that "emptiness" means things cannot function, then, with an improper understanding of the view of emptiness, one will have fallen into *nihilism*. So, because one has failed to reconcile emptiness and the fact that things work, this view is incorrect. That is why it is said that the meaning of emptiness is to be understood in terms of dependent arising.

Now, since the meaning of emptiness is to be explained in terms of dependent arising, we can only explain something as arising dependently if there is a basis, that is, some *thing* that *is* dependent. Hence, such a basis must exist. We see then that when we speak of dependent arising, we are indicating that things work. Dependent arising proves that things have no inherent existence, through the fact that things work in dependence on each other. The fact that things work and the fact that they do so in dependence, one on the other, eliminates the possibility of their being *independent*. This in turn precludes the possibility of inherent existence, since, to inherently exist means to be independent. Hence, the understanding of emptiness, of the emptiness of a kind of inherent existence that is independent, boils down to understanding dependent arising.

Now, just as we were able to deduce that things are empty from the fact that they arise dependently, likewise it is possible to understand dependent arising from the fact that things are empty. So, because things are empty, they function. This in turn implies that karma and its effects are operative, that we must know what to abandon and what to take up.

However, when we think deeply about emptiness, about the absence of inherent existence, when we search for the labeled object, "the self," among the aggregates, the self as it normally appears to us cannot be found. The self, as it arises in our everyday mind, cannot be found. This kind of self appears to us in this way as a result of our having been accustomed to seeing things as inherently existing since beginningless time. But such a self does not exist.

When we do perceive it, there is a danger that we may come to feel that it does not exist at all. It is helpful at this point to consider how it is that things, which even in common parlance are considered "false," exist, and how in regard to those things, their being false and their functioning do not contradict each other. For example, consider the reflection of a thing in a mirror. The reflection is in no way the thing which it appears to be. It is empty of being the thing in every respect. The reflection, or image, of the thing in the mirror is in every way, in every respect, empty of being the thing which it appears to be. Nonetheless, when the thing comes to be placed in front of the mirror, when the condition of the meeting of thing and mirror occurs, then, in spite of the fact that it is a false thing, the reflection appears. And when the thing is taken away, despite its having been a false thing all along, nonetheless the reflection disappears. This shows that a thing's being false does not preclude its working or functioning.

The above has been an analysis of how dependent arising can act as a proof for a thing's being empty of inherent existence. Hence the understanding of dependent arising has the capacity to eliminate both of the extremes (of eternalism and nihilism). When we search for the labeled object and do not find it, we conclude that there is no inherent existence, no essence. "If an essence existed, it should be found, but I have not found anything at all" — to proceed in this way alone is to get a one-sided understanding of emptiness, this is not

43

said to be a true kind of emptiness. The true kind of emptiness is the emptiness via dependent arising.

Now if this view of emptiness as it is explained by the
Ācāryas Buddhapālita and Candrakīrti (Prāsaṅgikas) does not
make sense to one, there is no point in forcing oneself to
accept it. Instead, one might find more acceptable the explanation of emptiness of true existence of the Sautrāntika school
which *nominally* accepts that a thing exists by virtue of its
own characteristic, leaving aside the (Prāsaṅgika) belief that
things only exist as linguistically labeled entities (that they
have no more existence than what is imparted to them by a
name). Again, one might find it more adequate to think of
things according to the views of the Cittamātra (Mind Only)
school. But whatever view one decides to adopt, one must
be sure that it is one which opposes or counteracts the negative emotions and the misapprehension of true existence. At
the same time, it must not contradict the fact that things
work, that they function interdependently. This is an extremely important point. And we should keep in mind that
if we find the first view unacceptable, we should think about
the other schools such as the Sautrāntika and Cittamātra as
possible alternatives.

It is necessary to come to an understanding of emptiness
by eliminating the two extremes (of eternalism and nihilism), and there are two separate means for doing this. The
extreme of eternalism, the misapprehended self, is eliminated
by reasoning. And it is chiefly one's own experience which

eliminates the extreme of nihilism. So when we are about to meditate on emptiness, be prepared to pinch your hand. If when you think you have understood emptiness, you come to believe that nothing exists, then give yourself a good pinch. It will be *that* experience which will eliminate the nihilistic view.

Question: **A Buddhist, as I understand it, is a person who is supposed to demonstrate compassion by working to eliminate the suffering of all sentient beings. Yet, quite often, the suffering of sentient beings is caused by other sentient beings. So, I'm wondering if it is possible that a Buddhist, in order to help the majority of sentient beings, might harm those who are causing this suffering to the majority. In other words, is it permissible for a Buddhist to harm someone in order to help others?**

His Holiness: This depends upon the situation — it must be examined. It depends upon the qualifications of the adept and upon the ramifications of the action.

For example, if someone is about to do a very sinful action, an action which will harm many people, then, in such a case, motivated by compassion, we should try to stop the action. If, however, there is no other alternative, if violence is the only option, if only that will stop the evil action, the misdeed, from being performed, then in such a case violence, a harsh counteraction, is both permissible and necessary. Superficially, though such counter-measures may appear to harm a particular person, because of our motivation and the virtuous nature of our ultimate aim, it is just as if we were administering a disciplinary punishment. It is not done through hatred, but it is only out of compassion and out of a desire to stop the evil deed that we apply this harsh method. The kind of parents who, motivated by a deep sense of sympathy toward their own children, will use harsh words or forceful, physical action to stop their children from misbehaving appear, superficially, to be harming the child by beating it, etc., but in reality, they are helping it. So, you see, there is no contradiction.

Question: **Could your Holiness explain the application of** *vipaśyanā* **in the Sūtra and Tantra Vehicles?**

His Holiness: What does *vipaśyanā* (*lhag mthong*) mean? It means to see (*mthong*) things in a better or superior way (*lhag par*). This is the etymology of the word. But what does it mean "to see things in a better way," you might ask. It means that, by the power of analysis or examination, one comes to see the aspect, or qualities, of an object in a better way by understanding that object with a form of analytical wisdom. Hence "vipaśyanā" is said to be a form of analytical meditation.

Now, one's own individual wisdom is analyzing or trying to get to the heart of its object, but this won't come about unless one's mind is settled. Hence what we call "vipaśyanā" is a form of analysis by one's own individual wisdom when it is accompanied, or aided, by śamatha, mental quiescence. This is called the union of śamatha and vipaśyanā.

In the Sūtra Vehicle, śamatha is accomplished by means of stabilizing meditation and vipaśyanā by means of analytical meditation. They are not distinguished or differentiated in terms of *what* object they hold, only in terms of *how* they hold it.

Now the Tantra Vehicle is said to be an especially efficacious form of practice because it has more and better ways for achieving this *samādhi*, the conjunction of śamatha and vipaśyanā.

Of the four classes of Tantra, the methods for accomplishing śamatha and vipaśyanā as explained in the three lower classes are the same as those explained in such (Sūtrayāna) texts as (Asaṅga's) *Śrāvakabhūmi*, etc. In the Anuttara-yoga Tantra system, however, there is a form of practice that involves fixing one's concentration on different sites within the body. By doing so, it is possible to bypass analytic meditation altogether. Simply by doing stabilizing meditation (by placing the mind on these centers), it is possible to attain vipaśyanā.

Question: As the spiritual path and practices develop, there is sometimes a wish and interest to take ordination as a monk or nun in one of the traditions. A man or a woman may get to that point, and then it can become somewhat of a dilemma, "Should I ordain or should I not?" Could your Holiness offer some advice on this?

His Holiness: The Buddha, you see, explained a whole variety of different ways, of different methods. For laymen and laywomen there is the lay *śīla*, or vows. At the same time there is a monastic śīla. But here, the most important thing is to determine what form of discipline is most suitable for oneself and to abide by it. We ourselves must make the final decision. We must judge and ask ourselves whether or not we can keep the vows we are thinking of taking. If there is hesitation as to whether or not we can keep the monk's vows, for example, then it is better not to take them but to remain as a layperson, abiding by the conduct that is prescribed in the vows of a layman or laywoman. Once one feels confident that one can abide by the monk's or nun's rules, then take them.

Question: **A person, particularly in the West, must have the foundation of humility, honesty, and an ethical way of life. Once one has this foundation, what else does Your Holiness suggest that one cultivate in one's life? What else is valuable and necessary to bring into one's life, if there is the foundation of virtue, ethics, and humility?**

His Holiness: The next thing to be cultivated is samādhi, or meditative stabilization. Śīla is a method to control oneself — it is a defensive action. Our actual enemy is ourselves. The afflictive emotions (pride, anger, and jealousy) are our real enemies. These are the real troublemakers, and they are to be found within ourselves. The actual practice of Dharma consists of fighting against these inner enemies.

As in any war, first we must have a defensive action, and in our spiritual fight against the negative emotions, śīla is our defense. Knowing that at first one is not fully prepared for offensive action, we first resort to defensive action and that means śīla. But once one has prepared one's defenses, and has become somewhat accustomed to śīla, then one must launch one's offensive. Here our main weapon is *prajñā*, or wisdom, or we can say vipaśyanā, this too is wisdom. This weapon of wisdom is like a bullet, or maybe even a rocket, and the rocket launcher is śamatha, or calm abiding. In brief, once you have a basis in morality or ethics, the next step is to train in mental stabilization, or śamatha, and eventually in wisdom.

Question: To what do you attribute the growing fascination in the West, especially in America, with Eastern religions? I include many, many cults and practices which are becoming extremely strong in America. To what do you attribute, in this particular age, the reasons for this fascination, and would you encourage people who are dissatisfied with their own Western way of life, having been brought up in the Mosaic religions (Christianity, Judaism, and Islam), dissatisfied with their lack of spiritual refreshment, would you encourage them to search further in their own religions or to look into Buddhism as an alternative?

His Holiness: That's a tricky question. Of course, from the Buddhist viewpoint, we are all human beings, and we all have every right to investigate either our own religion or another religion. This is our right. I think that on the whole, a comparative study of different religious traditions is useful.

I generally believe that every major religion has the potential for giving any human being good advice; there is no question that this is so. But we must always keep in mind that different individuals have different mental predispositions. This means that for some individuals one religious system or philosophy will be more suitable than another. The only way one can come to a proper conclusion as to what is most suitable for *oneself* is through comparative study. Hence, we look and study, and we find a teaching that is most suitable to our own taste. This, you see, is my feeling.

I cannot advise everyone to practice Buddhism. That I cannot do. Certainly, for some people the Buddhist religion or ideology is most suitable, most effective. But that does not mean it is suitable for *all.*

The Third Discussion

At the outset, I would like to express my greetings. I am not staying many days in Bodhgaya, so I have been very busy. At the same time, there are many people this year, aren't there? There is a much bigger gathering this year than last year.

Now the teachings are finished and everyone is departing. Except for your memory, soon there will be nothing left of our days in Bodhgaya. This is the way of human life — time passes. As a Buddhist, one must think not only in terms of this lifetime, but in terms of trillions and trillions of years. To think in this way is also a form of practice. I think this is very important.

At the beginning, we must certainly learn from a teacher or from books. Then it is necessary to apply what we have learned to the new experiences and events we encounter in our daily lives. Now, in the present case, if we consider our departure from Bodhgaya, some people may feel sad. To dwell on this and to think: "Now we are leaving and we shall not see each other any longer" is not a very useful thing to do.

If, however, we contemplate the deeper significance, the implicit lesson in impermanence, the meaning of change, and the nature of human life, then the experience of departing can be a useful one. It becomes meaningful. Physically, we may be departing, but mentally, our memory and certain things we may have experienced in Bodhgaya, these will remain in our minds. The physical part cannot remain with you always. It will remain for a while and then depart. So, you see, all external material things, no matter how important or how beautiful, will eventually depart. But certain things which are related mainly to consciousness, to the inner experience, these, generally speaking, remain with you always.

Question: **Your Holiness, how can we separate the essence of Buddhism from Tibetan cultural adaptations?**

His Holiness: I think the basic teachings such as the Four Noble Truths, and the Two Truths (conventional and ultimate) are the very foundation of Buddhism. These are the teachings that are to be found in Indian Buddhism, Japanese Buddhism, Chinese, Thai, Burmese, and also in Tibetan Buddhism. They all have teachings such as the Four Noble Truths — these are basic to all forms of Buddhism. Now the Tantras are not practiced in common. They are practiced only in Tibet, in Japan, and perhaps in Korea. But we can nonetheless consider the Tantric teachings as authentic Buddhism, as the true teachings.

When we perform certain kinds of prayers and rituals in Tibetan Buddhism, in certain minor aspects, there may be Tibetan adaptations. These parts, then, can be dispensed with in the transmission of Buddhism to other cultures. For example, when we perform certain *pūjas* (offering rituals), we use certain musical instruments. We use, for example, the conch shell: this is something we took from India. (In Tibet, there were no conches, but other instruments were common.) When you Westerners perform these pūjas, these rituals, it is not necessary for you to use these same instruments, you can use your own.

This is just one example of aspects that are local adaptations. In another place with a different culture and different people, these things may not be relevant; they may not actually be useful, and that part should change. In the West, for example, there exists the tradition of using song; some Christians use song as a means of conveying and appreciating spiritual meaning. This is fine; it is useful.

Question: In the teachings there are many things mentioned that are contradicted by Western science. For example, it is claimed that the moon is one hundred miles above the earth, etc. Many of our teachers hold these views to be literally true and Western science to be wrong. Would Your Holiness comment on how we should view these teachings of the Buddha and on how we should regard our teachers who hold them literally?

His Holiness: This is a complicated matter. But I believe, and I have expressed this on several occasions, that basically a Buddhist attitude on any subject must be one that accords with the facts. If, upon investigation, you find that there is reason and proof for a point, then you should accept it. That is not to say that there are certain points that are beyond the human powers of deductive reasoning — that is a different matter. But things such as the size or position of the moon and stars, etc. are things that the human mind can come to know. On these matters it is important to accept the facts, the real situation, whatever it may be.

When we investigate certain measures and descriptions as they exist in our own texts, we find that they do not correspond to reality. In such a case, we must accept the reality and not the literal scriptural explanation. This should be the basic attitude.

If something is contradictory to reasoning, or if it is found to be false after investigation, then that point cannot be accepted. That is the rule, that is the general attitude. For example, if something is directly experienced by the senses, then there is no question, no doubt, that we should accept it.

In the scriptures there are many different cosmological theories expounded. We do believe that there are many billions and billions of worlds, in the same way that Western science accepts there are limitless numbers of galaxies. This is something that is mentioned very clearly in scripture, though the size and shape may not be the same. They may be different.

For example, Mt. Meru is mentioned in the scriptures. It is claimed to be the center of the earth. But if it is there, by following the description in scripture of its location, it must be found. At least we must get some indication that it is there, but there is none. So we must take a different interpretation from the literal one.

If there are teachers who still hold to the literal meaning, than that is their own business. There is no need to argue with them. You can see things according to your own interpretation, and they can see things as they see fit.

In any case, these are basically minor matters, aren't they? The foundation of the teachings — the Four Noble Truths, what they have to say about the nature of life, about the nature of suffering, about the nature of mind — these are the basic teachings, these are what is most important, what is relevant to our lives. Whether the world is square or round does not matter as long as it remains a peaceful and good place.

Question: **Can Your Holiness comment on the power of a holy place such as Bodhgaya. What makes virtuous activities performed here more powerful and worthy of more merit?**

His Holiness: The fact that many holy beings, spiritually advanced practitioners, stay and practice in a certain place makes the atmosphere or environment of that place change. The place gets some imprint from the person.

Then, when another person who does not have much experience or spiritual development comes and remains in that place and practices, he or she can obtain certain special kinds of experience, though of course, the right type of motivation and certain karmic forces must also be present in the person as contributing factors for such an experience to come about.

According to the Tantric teachings, at important places there are non-human beings, like *ḍākinīs*, who have bodies that are much more subtle than those of humans. When great spiritual practitioners stay in a certain place and perform meditation and rituals there, that place becomes familiar to beings like *ḍākas* and *ḍākinīs*, so that they may inhabit the place and travel around it. As indications of this, sometimes one may notice an unusual noise or smell that seems to have no particular reason for existing. These are indications that some higher beings, different beings who have more experience, are inhabiting or traveling through that place. This could also act as a factor influencing whether or not a place is considered special.

In addition, as for Bodhgaya, we know that the Buddha himself must have chosen this place for a particular reason — this we believe. Due to the power of his prayer, later, when his followers actually come to this place, they may feel something — hence the power of the Buddha's prayer could also be a factor.

Perhaps we must take human psychological factors into account as well. For example, Mahāyāna Buddhists feel strongly toward Śākyamuni Buddha, toward Nāgārjuna, etc. In my own case, I have a strong feeling towards the Buddha, towards Nāgārjuna, Ārya Asaṅga, to all of these great beings. So when you stay at the place where these people were born and remained, then you feel something. If you use this feeling in the right way, that is fine, there is nothing wrong with that.

Question: **Could Your Holiness say something about growing open to one's own inner guru and also something about the absolute guru?**

His Holiness: In general, there is said to be an inner guru, an outer guru, and a secret guru. This is explained in different scriptures, and there are some slight differences in the way these concepts are interpreted or explained in Nyingma, Kagyu, Sakya, and Gelug (the four main orders of Tibetan Buddhism). Likewise, there are differences in the way the different sects explain the four types of maṇḍalas: outer, inner, secret, and the maṇḍala of reality (*de kho na nyid*).

The internal, or inner, guru is the innermost subtle consciousness of the guru. Now, that innermost subtle consciousness which your guru has is exactly similar to the innermost subtle consciousness you yourself have. What then is the difference between the two? The guru, who is in effect using this subtle consciousness in his practice, is actually experiencing it with awareness, so that the consciousness becomes a form of wisdom.

When we faint or when we are dying, we too experience that subtle consciousness. And although that consciousness is there, although it is present, we are not aware or conscious of it. We do not realize that it is present. So the real guru, the inner guru, is this consciousness that exists within ourselves. It is also the inner protector, the real, ultimate refuge. It is the experience of that state that *is* the real teacher, that *is* the real protector, that *is* the real Dharma. Thus there is this inner guru.

Now, you see, we call the manifestation of that consciousness in the form of a human body the external guru.

As for the secret guru, it is the special method, or way, that brings us to an awareness of that consciousness. This includes the meditation on the channels and the winds. It includes breathing meditations, the generation of bliss, and developing the inner heat. These techniques we call the secret guru because it is through them that we come to realize the inner guru. Sometimes this subtle consciousness is called the "inner guru," sometimes it is called the "ultimate guru." In any case, the two terms are synonymous.

According to the sūtras, according to the Madhyamaka school, "the absolute" refers to *śūnyatā*, to emptiness. In the Anuttarayoga Tantras, however, the word "absolute" has two meanings. It can refer either to śūnyatā itself or to this special type of subtle consciousness (not to the ordinary, vulgar levels of mind however). For the most part, when these scriptures refer to "the ultimate," they are referring to the consciousness aspect, but not to ordinary consciousness, to a consciousness we call *rig pa*, the ultimate, innermost subtle consciousness. Even when the five senses are not active, the subtle consciousness is still there, though normally it is over-powered by the senses.

You see, all the senses are individual types of consciousnesses. The eye consciousness has color, shape, and so forth as its object; the ear consciousness perceives sounds, etc. Even though they are all different, having different objects, none-theless, they are all of the same nature, of the nature of know-ing. They may come to know through different means, but they are still of the nature of knowing. This aspect they have in common we call *shes pa*, knowing. Now the rig pa, which we can call "awareness," this innermost subtle consciousness, is also of the nature of "knowing." It too is a "knower," just as the eye consciousness is a "knower." So both the coarser sense consciousnesses and the more subtle rig pa are of the nature of knowing. They are both "knowers." The coarser types of consciousness come to know something because of the subtle consciousness. The basic nature of knowing thus comes from, or is due to, the existence of the subtle con-sciousness. Even during moments when the sense organs are very active, if we rely on the instructions of a proper, experi-enced teacher, we can separate the two experiences: the path of the coarser consciousnesses from the path of the subtle consciousness.

These points, however, are difficult. First of all, the mat-ter being discussed is difficult; add to that the fact that the Dalai Lama's English is poor, and it makes for an altogether awkward situation.

You see, it is actually quite shameful. For quite a few years now I have had to speak with my own English, but it never comes out properly. In fact, sometimes, instead of getting better, it actually declines!

Question: **Your Holiness, in what way does an individual consciousness exist? What part of that consciousness is still present after death? And is there a total dissolution of that consciousness when one reaches Buddhahood?**

His Holiness: Consciousness will always be present, though a particular consciousness may cease. For example, the particular tactile consciousness that is present within this human body will cease when the body comes to an end. Likewise, consciousnesses that are influenced by ignorance, by anger, or by attachment these too will cease. Furthermore, all of the coarser levels of consciousness will cease. But the basic, ultimate, innermost subtle consciousness will always remain. It has no beginning, and it will have no end. That consciousness will remain. When we reach Buddhahood, that consciousness becomes enlightened, all-knowing. Still, the consciousness will remain an individual thing. For example, the Buddha Śākyamuni's consciousness and the Buddha Kāśyapa's consciousness are distinct individual things. This individuality of consciousness is not lost upon the attainment of Buddhahood. Still, all of the minds of all Buddhas have the same qualities — in this sense they are similar. They have the same qualities while still preserving their individuality.

Question: **What does Your Holiness think of unilateral nuclear disarmament?**

His Holiness: Now, you see, world peace through mental peace is an absolute. It is the ultimate goal. But as for the method, there are many factors that must be taken into consideration. Under a particular set of circumstances, a certain approach may be useful while under other circumstances, another may be more useful. This is a very complicated issue which compels us to study the situation at a particular point of time. We must take into account the other side's motivation, etc., so it is a very complex matter.

But we must always keep in mind that all of us want happiness. War, on the other hand, only brings suffering — *that* is very clear. Even if we are victorious, that victory means sacrificing many people. It means their suffering. Therefore, the important thing is peace. But how do we achieve peace? Is it done through hatred, through extreme competition, through anger? It is obvious that through these means it is impossible to achieve any form of lasting world peace. Hence, the only alternative is to achieve world peace through mental peace, through peace of mind. World peace is achieved based only on a sense of brotherhood and sisterhood, on the basis of compassion. The clear, genuine realization of the oneness of all mankind is something important. It is something we definitely need. Wherever I go, I always express these views.

Question: Western monks and nuns sometimes find it difficult wearing robes in the West. We are often stared at and looked upon as being strange. Does Your Holiness recommend wearing robes in non-Buddhist countries?

His Holiness: This we must judge according to particular cases and circumstances. If you can remain in robes without disturbing others, then of course it is better to wear robes. In some particular cases, however, this may be difficult.

Basically, as practitioners, we must remain in society. We must be good members of the society in which we live. So if society has a negative attitude towards you, this may be good neither for yourself nor for society. This is our basic position. Now, if for this reason, one decides not to wear robes, if it is not suitable, better not to do so under those circumstances. This is all right. If the circumstances should change, then change. Gradually the society itself may change its attitudes. The West is a society in which Buddhism has never flourished, and this is changing. I think that, compared to thirty years ago, today when monks travel on an international air carrier, they are recognized as monks. So, you see, time goes on, and gradually things will change.

The important thing is not what we wear, but our behavior in our everyday lives.

Thank you very much. Today there is not much time, but I am happy to have shared these few moments with you. All of us have come from different parts of the world, and we may even have different faiths, but we all have the same human mind. Isn't that so? When it comes down to the level of basic human qualities, we are the same; there are no differences. So what we need to do is to go to a deeper level. There we find that we are all human brothers and sisters. No barriers exist for us. Everyone wants happiness and does not want suffering, and everyone has the right to achieve permanent happiness. So we must share each other's suffering and help each other. If we cannot help others, at least we must not harm them. That is the main principle. Whether we believe in the next life or not does not matter. Whether we believe in God or not doesn't matter. But, one thing that *does* matter very much is that we live peacefully, calmly, with a real sense of brotherhood and sisterhood. This is the way to achieve true world peace, or if not world peace, then at least a peaceful community. That is very important, very useful, and very helpful. Thank you very much.

The Fourth Discussion

Question: **The Christian notion of God is that He is omni-scient, all-compassionate, all-powerful, and the Creator. The Buddhist notion of Buddha is the same, except that He is not the Creator. To what extent does the Buddha exist apart from our minds, as the Christians believe their God to?**

His Holiness: There are two ways of interpreting this question. The general question is whether the Buddha is a separate thing from mind. Now in one sense, this could be asking whether or not the Buddha is a phenomenon imputed or labeled by mind, and of course, all phenomena in this sense must be said to be labeled by name and conceptual thought. The Buddha is not a separate phenomenon from mind because our minds impute or label him by means of words and conceptual thought.

In another sense, the question could be asking about the relationship of Buddhahood to our own minds, and in this sense we must say that Buddhahood, or the state of being a Buddha, is the object to be attained by us. Buddhahood is the resultant object of refuge. Our minds are related to Buddhahood (they are not separate from Buddhahood) in the sense that this is something that we will gradually attain by the systematic purification of our minds. Hence, by purifying our minds step by step, we will eventually attain the state of Buddhahood. And that Buddha which we will eventually become is of the same continuity as ourselves. But that Buddha which we will become is different, for example, from Śākyamuni Buddha. They are two distinct persons. We cannot attain Śākyamuni Buddha's enlightenment, because that is his own individual thing.

If, instead, the question is referring to whether or not our minds are separate from the state of Buddhahood, and if we take Buddhahood to refer to the essential purity of the mind, then, of course this is something which we possess even now. Even today, our minds have the nature of essential purity. This is something called the "buddha nature." The very nature of the mind, the mere quality of knowledge and clarity without being affected by conceptual thoughts, that too we may call "buddha nature." To be exact, it is the innermost clear light mind which is called the "buddha nature."

Question: **When creating merit, one must acknowledge that Christians create merit as well as Buddhists, so that the whole source of merit cannot reside solely in the object, i.e. Buddha or God, to which one is making offerings. This**

leads me to think that the source of merit is in our own minds. Could you please comment on this?

His Holiness: The main thing is motivation, but probably there *is* some difference in regard to the object to which one makes offerings and so forth. The pure motivation must, however, be based on reasoning, that is, it must be verified by valid cognition; it must be unmistaken. But no doubt that the main point is the motivation.

For example, when we generate great compassion, we take as our object sentient beings. But it is not due to anything on the side of the sentient beings, on the part of the sentient beings, that great compassion is special. It is not due to any blessing from sentient beings that great compassion is special. Nonetheless, when we meditate in this way on great compassion and we generate it from our hearts, we know that there is a tremendous amount of benefit that results from this. This is not however, due to anything from the side of sentient beings, from the object of the great compassion. It is simply by thinking of the kindness of sentient beings and so forth that we generate great compassion and that benefit comes, but not due to the blessing of (or anything inherent in) sentient beings themselves. So strictly from the point of view of motivation, from one's own motivation, a great amount of benefit can result, isn't it so?

Likewise, when we take the Buddha as our object, if our motivation is that of great faith, of very strong faith, and we make offerings and so forth, then again, great benefit can result from this. Although a suitable object is necessary, that is, an object which, for example, has limitless good qualities, nonetheless the principal thing is our motivation, i.e., the strong faith. Still there is probably some difference as regards the kind of object to which one is making these offerings.

From one point of view, were sentient beings not to exist, then we could not take them as our object, and great compassion could not arise. So from this perspective, the object is, once again, very important. If suffering sentient beings did not exist, compassion could never arise. So from that point of view, the object, sentient beings, is a special one.

Question: **Concepts are always arising in the mind. Could His Holiness please explain how to meditate so as to liberate the mind from concepts?**

His Holiness: As regards the cessation of concepts, when the mind is settled in single-pointed equipoise on an object, at that time, certain kinds of concepts or misconceptions cease. They are prohibited from arising. But this does nothing more than to close the door on the conceptions, for as soon as we come out of this state, then the conceptions come racing back into the mind. The conceptions are just waiting outside the door, and when we open it, they come running back in. It is at most a temporary relief. It's like taking an aspirin for a headache. To bring an end to misconception from the root, i.e., totally, the method consists of the cultivation of wisdom. And this refers specifically to perceiving emptiness; it means meditating on emptiness.

Even though they have completely eliminated all afflictive emotions, or *kleśas*, Śrāvaka and Pratyekabuddha Arhants have dualistic misconceptions, do they not? Likewise, even in the Mahāyāna, the eighth, ninth, and tenth-stage Boddhisattvas have also rid themselves of the afflictive emotions. Nonetheless, they still have conceptions. So until one attains Buddhahood, except for the times when one is engaged in single-pointed equipoise on emptiness, at all other times, dualistic conceptions exist. Until the attainment of Buddhahood, one proceeds by alternating periods of equipoise and post-attainment, then another period of equipoise followed by another of post-attainment and so forth. Until one attains Buddhahood, one is under the influence of the obscurations to knowledge, and this refers specifically to the obscuration of seeing the Two Truths as being of different natures. This is the explanation according to the Sūtra system.

If one explains it according to the Tantras, specifically, if one explains it according to the Guhyasamāja Tantra, until one attains the subtlest clear light, until that point, one still continues to suffer from dualistic appearances. But when one abides in the subtlest clear light, at that point things cease to appear as dual. When one brings an end to the obscurations to knowledge, i.e. to those things which block our knowing all phenomena, then one brings an end to the appearance that the Two Truths are of different natures. And when this stain which apprehends the Two Truths to be of different natures ceases, then, without having to perceive the subject (a chair say), that subject's reality, or nature, i.e. emptiness, can be perceived. It can be perceived directly. We can see that in such an equipoise on emptiness the subject is itself directly perceived. So from this point on, the stain of dualistic appearances is destroyed from the root and one can say that all conceptions cease beyond this point. In such an equipoise on emptiness, conventional phenomena are perceived directly. That very mind which directly perceives emptiness itself directly perceives conventional phenomena. Hence, at that time there is no conceptual thought. This is a very difficult point.

The word "conception," in Tibetan *rtog pa,* can have many different meanings. For example, there are mistaken conceptions, *log rtog,* there are misconceptions which apprehend existence, *bden 'dzin gyi rtog pa,* etc. These are things which are to be eliminated, which harm the individual. However, there is a sense of the word "conception" which is not negative. The appearance of conventional phenomena is a good example. Conceptions in regard to conventional phenomena are not things which harm us. They are not interferences. So we have to be aware that there are these different connotations of the word "conception." For example, we normally have conceptions of the sort: "this is like this" or "this is like that." These kinds of conceptions do not harm us in any way, do they?

Question: Would His Holiness please give reasons why the mental consciousness is not the person?

His Holiness: Now, among the tenets of Buddhism there are schools which accept consciousness to be the person, to exemplify the person. For example, the Ācārya Bhāvaviveka accepts this position. He is a great Mādhyamika, is he not? He even looked down somewhat upon the Ācārya Buddhapālita, who is considered one of the seniormost followers of the protector Nāgārjuna.

Following the Ācārya Buddhapālita, there was Ācārya Candrakīrti, who was a Prāsaṅgika. Now, according to the Prāsaṅgika school, consciousness is "that which knows." It is the "knower." If one were going to posit the consciousness to be the "self," then it would only make sense to posit the most subtle consciousness to be the self, or an example of the self, which is to say that only the subtlest consciousness as it is explained in the tantras would be an adequate candidate. It would make no sense to posit the rougher levels of consciousness to be the self, because in states such as the equipoise of the cessation of consciousness, all of the rough levels of consciousness are eliminated. It is for this reason that some accept the *ālaya vijñāna*, the foundation consciousness, to be the self, for at the times that the rougher levels of consciousness cease, the ālaya vijñāna, the foundation consciousness, does not. Hence, they see a need for setting aside one consciousness which is more subtle than the other grosser levels and which remains even at the time that those rougher levels cease. They claim that this subtler level, the foundation consciousness, is the self. So, logically, if one were to posit a form of consciousness to be an example of the self, to *be* the self, then it would make no sense *but* to posit the most subtle consciousness to be that example of self.

Now, that entity, that phenomenon, which engages in the action of "knowing," which is of the nature of knowledge, this is what is called "consciousness." If we claim that this is the self, it would follow, absurdly, that the actor and the action, the doer of the action and the action itself would become identical. Based on the action of "knowing," we say such expressions as "I know." So, if the self were not different from the "knowing," then expressions like "I know" would be meaningless, would they not?

What is more, if the consciousness were posited as an example of the self, then when we search for the labeled object, the self, there would be something that would be found, would there not? This, of course, is not possible.

But chiefly, the argument is as before: that in conventional expressions, such as "my body," "my speech," "my mind," etc., we notice that there is implicit within these expressions an experiencer or an owner, which is the self, which makes use of or which possesses the five aggregates, including consciousness. Hence, consciousness is that which belongs to, or which is made use of by, the self and is not, therefore, the self. There is probably more to be said in this regard, but this is what comes to mind at the moment.

Question: **Even if one's guru is widely disparaged and criticized by other people, if, however, one sees no fault in this guru, is there any reason to lose faith in him?**

His Holiness: This is a complicated matter, a difficult problem. Before one recognizes someone as one's own lama or as a guru, it is necessary to investigate this person thoroughly. It is possible to get teachings from people without recognizing them as one's gurus. One can simply regard them as Dharma-friends and learn from them, go to teachings, and so forth. It is, however, impossible to receive initiations from them unless one considers them gurus. It is impossible to receive an initiation while simply regarding them as Dharma-friends. It is necessary to consider them as gurus. However, it is possible to receive general teachings from someone without considering him or her to be one's spiritual master.

Before creating a dharmic connection with someone, it is necessary to listen to criticism well. It is necessary to examine and analyze things well.

Once, however, one has taken initiation from a spiritual master, then the relationship of guru-disciple has been established and even if one later thinks that it was too premature a move, nonetheless, the relationship has been set. So at that time, it is better not to listen to criticism and instead simply to go on one's own way without listening to disparaging claims being made about one's own spiritual master. It is better at that time to have a neutral attitude, without thinking that the criticism that has been offered is good, without thinking that it is bad, instead, one should remain neutral.

From another viewpoint, it may be possible to separate, or make distinct, the source of one's faith in the guru, and yet recognize the fact that he or she may still have certain faults. For example, we may receive a certain Dharma teaching from a certain guru, and it is because we have received such a teaching from such a person that he or she is for us a source of respect and faith. There is no need to even question this fact. If, however, our gurus, in their day-to-day activities, should suffer from certain types of faults, then it is necessary to accept that in reality they do suffer from these faults. So if they have these, we should recognize them as faults. But this does not repudiate the fact that we may still have great faith and devotion in them in so far as they are the source of Dharma teachings. So it is possible to have this more realistic type of attitude in which we can both identify and recognize the faults of our spiritual master and yet have great respect and faith in them. In general, however, the best thing is to be cautious *before* we receive teachings.

Question: **One renowned vipaśyanā teacher of the Theravada tradition has said that for the attainment of enlightenment, mantras are useless. They may stimulate your cakras and bring about feelings of bliss, but for the attainment of full** enlightenment, they are useless. If you meditate with mantras, it is much easier to pass hours without much discomfort, for the mind is distracted.

Then he said that visualizations cannot lead us to enlightenment because by visualizations we are creating an illusion and then making that illusion part of ourselves. Therefore, we are only adding illusions to illusions and not coming to understand reality.

My question is, from the point of view of the Secret Mantra, of Tantra, what are the benefits and the purpose of mantra recitation and visualization?

His Holiness: This is an excellent question. In fact, it is one that was raised during ancient times by great scholars in India. Now the word "mantra" is sometimes taken to refer only to mantra repetition, but it can also be used as a synonym for Tantra. So let's leave that aside for the moment and instead focus on the actual, essential, or root meaning, of Tantra, that is, that which is actually meditated upon in Tantra.

Now in this regard, the Ācārya Buddhajñāna raised the following question. He said that apart from the misconception which is the apprehension of true existence, there is no other thing which can be said to be the root of saṃsāra, of cyclic existence. He said, therefore, that the antidote which can cut the root of saṃsāra must be a mind which opposes, which is in opposition to, this apprehension of true existence. That mind which acts as an antidote in the elimination of the root of saṃsāra must have as its object something which is in contradiction to, or which opposes, the object of true grasping, namely, true existence. Therefore, as an antidote to this root of saṃsāra, the apprehension of a self, it is necessary to apply a mind which has as its object the antithesis of this, namely, selflessness. Then the objection is raised that in the stage of generation when one meditates on the body of a deity, that this prerequisite is not fulfilled, i.e. that this (deity yoga) alone cannot lead us to an understanding or a realization of selflessness, and that therefore meditation on the stage of generation, Tantric meditation, cannot cut the root of saṃsāra.

The Ācārya Buddhajñāna answered this objection in this way. He said that in the meditation or visualization of deities, the realization of emptiness was indeed included. He said that tantric meditation included, that *it was* in fact, the realization of emptiness. How is this so? It is so because one takes as the perceived object, that is, as the referent object, the deity's body, but one perceives the deity's body as *having the aspect or quality of essencelessness*. For example, when one meditates on the emptiness of a sprout, the sprout is the subject or the referent object, and the emptiness is the aspect or quality. Likewise, in this case, the deity's body is the referent object and the aspect is emptiness. One meditates on that body in the aspect of, or having the quality of, emptiness.

Now what is the difference between these two types of mind: one which realizes the emptiness of a sprout, the other which realizes the emptiness of the deity's body in deity visualization? In the former case, the object, the sprout, is something which comes about in dependence upon certain actions and causes. It is an external thing. In the latter case, however, the deity's body is something that is simply conjured up in the mind of the yogi. The sprout is a factual thing. The deity is only a visualization. This is the difference. Now the aspect in both cases is the same; it is the emptiness, the absence of true existence, but because the subjects are different, the sprout in one case, the visualized deity's body in the other, there is a difference as to the degree of difficulty in ascertaining the emptiness of these two different objects. For example, there is also a difference in the degree of difficulty in coming to understand the emptiness of the person and the emptiness of the aggregates (the former being easier to understand).

In the process of coming to understand the emptiness of the sprout, the appearance of the sprout itself begins to wane as one comes to understand its emptiness, so that finally, when one comes to understand the emptiness of the sprout, the non-inherent existence of the sprout, the sprout itself does not appear at all. In Tantra, however, a special effort is made so that the referent object, the deity's body, does not disappear when its aspect, the emptiness, is realized. Hence, in the case of Tantra, when we realize the non-true existence, or non-inherent existence of the deity's body, the deity's body at that time does not disappear, but instead remains. Now, we mentioned that in the case of Tantra there is a special effort made to preserve not only the ascertainment or the realization of the emptiness of the deity's body, but also the appearance of the deity's body itself. In the case of the sprout, in the non-Tantric case, there is no such special effort made to preserve the appearance of the sprout. In fact, there is no need to preserve the appearance of the sprout, but there is a reason for trying to preserve the appearance of the deity's body when the emptiness of that deity's body is ascertained, and it is this.

In general, there are two accumulations: the accumulation of merit and the accumulation of wisdom. In order to obtain omniscience, it is necessary to obtain both the *rūpakāya*, or form body, and the *dharmakāya*, or phenomenal body. And for this, it is necessary to complete the two accumulations of merit and wisdom respectively. Now, in the Sūtra Vehicle, when we take the Buddha's body or status as an object, and prostrate to it, we accumulate merit. So, at the time that the Buddha's body is serving as the object of our prostration, at that very time, it can appear as if it were an illusion, but we cannot ascertain the lack of true existence of an object in regard to it, for as soon as that is ascertained, the appearance of the Buddha statue would vanish. So, in the Sūtra system, it is impossible to perceive the lack of true existence of an object at the same time that we are generating merit in regard to it. In the Sūtra system, the generation of merit and wisdom are two separate actions that must be done at two separate times. They involve two different minds.

In the Tantra, however, it is a single mind that accomplishes both actions. Taking the body of a deity as the referent object, we achieve the accumulation of merit. At the same time, realizing that the aspect, or quality, of that deity's body is emptiness, the lack of true existence, we accomplish the accumulation of wisdom. These are both achieved simultaneously.

There is an additional difference insofar as the Buddha statue in the first case is a factual, external thing, whereas the deity's body in the Tantric case is something that is created, or imagined, within the mind of the yogi who is doing Tantric practice. In fact, according to worldly parlance, one would almost say that a visualized image is not a true thing. In any case, the visualized image is more subtle.

What is more, when we do deity visualization, it is not just done at random. Instead, the deity's body is generated from within the sphere of emptiness. And what this means is that first one meditates on emptiness as well as one can, to the level of one's ability, and then from within the sphere of that understanding of emptiness, one comes to visualize the deity's body.

These, then, are the main reasons for how and why the practice of emptiness is contained within the Tantric path, and why the Tantric vehicle therefore has the ability to destroy the root of saṃsāra. In the Sūtrayāna, we speak of a wisdom that is seized or grasped by method, or a method that is grasped, or seized by wisdom. But in the Tantric path, there is *one* mind, one *single* mind, which accomplishes both the accumulation of merit and wisdom simultaneously. This one mind has the ability both to accumulate merit *and* to accumulate wisdom. And hence in the Tantra, we do not speak of wisdom seizing merit or merit seizing wisdom, but simply of one mind which accomplishes both. If we test and experiment with regard to these points, we will find out for ourselves whether or not there is in fact a difference between meditation in the Sūtra system and in the Tantric system.

From another point of view, there is also a difference in the Sūtrayāna and the Tantrayāna insofar as in the latter it is possible to accomplish the four kinds of attainments: the extraordinary attainments such as the powers of peace, increase, power, and wrath. By the visualization of the deity and the maṇḍala, one can achieve certain attainments such as long life, the increase of wisdom, and so forth.

In addition, there is also a difference between Sūtra and Tantra in regard to the quality of the one-pointedness of mind. For example, in the special case of the Anuttarayoga Tantra, there is a type of meditation on the winds, the channels, and so forth. In the system of the perfections, in the Sūtrayāna, vipaśyanā (insight) is explained to be a strictly analytical type of meditation, whereas śamatha (calm abiding) is explained to be a strictly stabilizing type of meditation. But in the Anuttarayoga Tantra system, because there is a difference in the method of meditation, simply by means of stabilizing meditation, one can attain vipaśyanā. So in the Anuttarayoga

Tantra system, by meditating on the winds and the channels, etc., it is possible to achieve vipaśyanā simply by a stabilizing, or equipoise, type of meditation.

Why is this so? Normally, unless one analyzes something, the object does not become clear. The purpose of analyzing something is so that it becomes clearer. In the Tantrayāna, however, by means of meditation on the winds and the channels, due to a physical condition, the mind becomes more and more subtle by means of stabilizing methods, i.e. methods in which the mind becomes clearer and clearer, so that even without investigation, simply through the method of one-pointed concentration, one can achieve vipaśyanā.

Now, there are not too many people who have achieved results, but there are a few who, practicing in accordance with these principles, have in fact been able to verify this. So you see, it has been proven. This question is a very important one.

Question: **When non-Buddhist friends and one's parents are curious about one's purpose for spending time in retreat and study instead of getting involved "in the world," what does Your Holiness feel is the best line of reasoning to use in order to help them understand something they might find incomprehensible?**

His Holiness: I think that depends upon the individual case. You see, we have to consider the actual situation. If the parent is a very religious-minded person, one can explain it to them in one way. If they are not religious-minded, if they are only thinking in terms of material values, if they have a materialistic outlook on life, then of course it is necessary to explain it to them in a different way. In any case, I think you know better how to answer this question (pointing to the Western monks).

Question: **If you want to take them in the West, are the Mahāyāna Precepts fixed rules, or are they more a training for the mind? Can lunch break, for example, be taken at one p.m.? Is it possible to take precepts if one has to take lunch at one p.m.? Does one have to take all eight, or can one take as many as one wants? Do intoxicants refer to cigarettes? And, what kinds of food is one not allowed to eat?**

His Holiness: As regards the time after which food is prohibited, in general, this is to be gauged by the position of the sun when it reaches mid-point in the sky wherever one is living. The rule on eating before twelve noon, then, means that one should eat before that time. If, after having taken the vows, one finds one cannot eat before that time, then there is nothing to be done, is there? If originally one takes the vow, thinking that one can do it, and if an exceptional circumstance arises and one is not able to eat before that time, then what can be done? If one originally thinks, "I will definitely eat before mid-day," but due to one circumstance or another on is unable to do so, then it is necessary to make an exception for oneself, isn't it so? In general, one should refrain from all intoxicants, and although cigarette smoking is not specifically mentioned, still it is better if one does not smoke cigarettes during this time. So, although it is better to stop, still one must judge the actual circumstances for oneself. For example, if one is the kind of person who cannot stand being without a cigarette for a day, if not smoking will make one unable to think or act, then it is better if one smokes, isn't it? Therefore, if, with sincere motivation, in order to practice better during the day, one smokes, then it's all right to smoke one or two. I think it's all right. The main point is that we must look to the result or the value of the actions.

In general, an action may be negative, but under a particular set of circumstances it may be necessary to do it. If one cannot practice in a more extensive way, then it may be necessary to make exceptions. In Buddhism there are no absolutes.

For example, killing is very bad. This is something which we believe in Buddhism. We believe in non-violence one hundred percent. But there are many different degrees and levels of violence and non-violence. With bad motivation, to show kindness is not good. If one's ultimate goal or aim is to mislead someone, then showing them kindness with such an ulterior motive is a most evil deed. This is the worst kind of violence, isn't it? On the other hand, if with a very good motivation, in order to prevent someone from coming to harm, one acts in a rough or violent way, or acts rudely, apparently it is violence, but in reality, ultimately, it is permissible.

So under changing circumstances, these rules may change. The one principle which should not change under any circumstances is the principle of helping others. But, the way of helping others — this way in certain circumstances, another way in another set of circumstances — may change.

In general, it is stated that one should also be vegetarian during the day when one takes the Mahāyāna Precepts. One should refrain from taking animal products.

Question: **In order to realize the truth spoken of by the Buddha, is it necessary to be in a retreat situation, or can one realize it by doing work of a helping nature in the community? And what is the relative importance of both kinds of situations?**

His Holiness: In general, if one can do *both*, it is best. I think this is the practical way to do it; for the greatest part of the year, we have to live in society, we have to lead a good life. We have to live properly, and be an honest, sincere human being. But for a few weeks, or two months, or three months, to make retreat, to forget other worldly business and to concentrate solely on one's practice, I think this is the best way. If, however, someone has a special vocation for the eremitic life, if someone has a talent for living and practicing in isolation and can make a special effort to achieve good results, then of course it is a different question. Then it may be worthwhile to live in complete isolation and to put all of one's energies toward practicing. But this is the exception and quite rare. I think that among one million people, there may be one or two with this type of talent or vocation.

Question: **Is basic consciousness permanent and independent? Is anything permanent and independent?**

His Holiness: Consciousness is eternal. Its continuity never ceases. But it is not permanent. Permanence refers to the fact that something does not change from moment to moment. And this, of course, consciousness *does do*. It is impermanent in this sense, but it is still eternal. The continuity of the moments never ceases.

Question: **When meditating on consciousness, can one penetrate or go any further into consciousness than merely being aware of that consciousness?**

His Holiness: In general, it is first necessary to understand the conventional nature of consciousness. By concentrating on the mind, one can come to understand the nature of mind. And once this is ascertained, once this becomes clear to oneself, then one can concentrate on the ultimate nature, the ultimate reality of the mind.

The Fifth Discussion

Question: **How does one practice guru devotion, and how does one purify non-virtuous actions created towards one's guru?**

His Holiness: A common method of practicing guru devotion is to visualize one's guru, and to recite his name-mantra (*mtshan sngags*) or the hundred syllable mantra (*yig brgya*). For purification of non-virtuous actions accumulated with regard to one's guru, it is very good to do prostrations along with the recitation of the *Sūtra of Confession to the Thirty-five Buddhas.* This is a short sūtra and it has been translated into English. It is one very common practice. Then, also, one can perform the practice and recitation of Damtshig Dorje. The mantra itself is *Oṃ aḥ prajñādhrika ha hūṃ.* In any case, to recite these mantras is fine and it will help, but I think the most important thing is to practice the general teachings of

the Dharma sincerely. That is the principal method for purifying these non-virtues.

I have made the point in the past that it is not necessary to
consider someone one's guru from the very outset simply
because one has heard the explanation of the Buddha's teachings from that person. At first, it is much better if one does
not have that kind of attitude toward them, simply regarding them as a Dharma-friend. One gets teachings, and time
goes by. Then, when one feels that one knows that person
quite well, and can take them as one's guru without any danger of transgressing the commitments that accompany such
a relationship, when one has that kind of confidence, then
one can go ahead and take him or her as one's guru. The
Lord Buddha himself made it quite clear in both the Vinaya
sūtras and in the Mahāyāna scriptures, and even in the
Tantrayāna, in a very detailed fashion, what the qualities of a
teacher should be. This is why I often criticize the Tibetan
attitude of seeing whatever the guru does as good, of respecting everything that the guru does right from the start
without the initial period of examination. Of course, if the
guru is *really* qualified, then to have such an attitude is very
worthwhile.

Take the cases of Naropa and Marpa, for example. Sometimes it appears as though some of the things Tilopa asked of
Naropa, or Naropa of Marpa, were unreasonable. Deep down,
however, these requests had great meaning. Because of their
great faith in their gurus, Naropa and Marpa did as instructed.

Despite the fact that they *appeared* to be unreasonable, because the teachers were qualified, their actions had some meaning. In such situations, it is necessary that from the disciple's side all of the actions of the teacher be respected. But this cannot be compared to the case of ordinary people. Broadly speaking, I feel that the Buddha gave us complete freedom of choice to thoroughly examine the person who is to be our guru. This is very important. Unless one is definite, one should not take them as a guru. This preliminary examination is a kind of precautionary measure.

Question: **Could you please say something on the three kinds of suffering?**

His Holiness: One kind of suffering is like a headache or like yesterday's flu: discomfort in the nose, watery eyes, and so forth. In short, it includes all of those kinds of gross physical and mental sufferings that in ordinary parlance we usually call "suffering." This is the first category.

Then the second category is as follows. When we feel hungry and begin to take food, at first we feel very happy. We take one mouthful, then two, three, four, five... eventually, though it is the same person, the same food, and the same time period, we begin to find the food objectionable and reject it. This is what is meant by the "suffering of change." Practically every worldly happiness and pleasure is in this second category. Compared to other forms of suffering, at the beginning these more subtle forms of suffering seem pleasurable; they seem to afford us some happiness, but this is not true or lasting happiness, for the more we become acquainted with them, the more involved we become with them, the more suffering and trouble they bring us. That is the second category.

Now as for the third category, I think it is fair to say that it is one's own body. Roughly speaking, this is what it is. It is the body which is the fruit of afflictions, a body originally created by afflictions. Because the body is created by such causes, it is of the very nature of suffering. It comes to act as the basis of suffering. This then is the third category.

Even animals have the desire to overcome the first kind of suffering. The second category of suffering is something both Buddhists and non-Buddhists seek to overcome. With the practice of samādhi (mental concentration) and a certain kind of vipaśyanā (insight), i.e. based on a path which possesses the aspects of śamatha (mental quiescence) and vipaśyanā, it is possible to accomplish this. You see, saṃsāra is divided into three realms, the *kāmadhātu* (realm of desire), *rūpadhātu* (realm of form), and *arūpadhātu* (formless realm). The lowest realm is the desire realm, then comes a realm with form, and finally a realm without form, a formless realm. So with śamatha and a kind of vipaśyanā which can make distinctions, which can discriminate between these different realms, which can determine that the lower realms are more troublesome, while the higher ones are comparatively more peaceful, with this and a great deal of effort at very deep meditation, one can create the karmic seeds for being reborn in an upper realm.

In these higher realms, there is no suffering of suffering, and, without going into details, let me just say that beyond a certain stage, there is no suffering of change. At this point, only the most basic suffering, the third category exists. As long as one remains in saṃsāra, the third kind of suffering will always be present. It is only when one gets rid of this third kind of suffering that one can be said to have attained Nirvāṇa. Within Buddhism itself, there are different ideas concerning this point. According to the lower schools, since the body itself is the basis of suffering, as long as it is present, so too is suffering. According to them, when the Buddha attained enlightenment in Bodhgaya, he overcame two evils: that of the hosts of demons led by Māra and that of the afflictive emotions, the kleśas. But, they continue, there were two more evils left to overcome: that of the body, and that of death. These, they say, were vanquished only at Kushinagari, with the Buddha's passing away. At that moment, the two evil forces of the body and of death were supposed to have been conquered. According to this school of thought, when a being, like Śākyamuni Buddha, attains *mahāparinirvāṇa* and passes away, he ceases to exist, there is no further continuity of consciousness. Therefore, according to the Vaibhāṣika school, for example, after this point there is no more being, no more consciousness. Only the name remains. And yet, they believe that this being who has now disappeared can influence the course of those who follow him due to the virtues that he created in the past.

This explanation is not accepted by the higher schools of thought, however. These schools instead believe that there are two kinds of bodies, those that are pure in nature and those that are impure. The latter is more gross, whereas a body that has been purified is more subtle. Now, for example, when Śākyamuni Buddha gave up his body, there still remained the more subtle one. So, according to these schools of thought, at the stage of Buddhahood, there are two bodies: a mental body and a physical one. I don't know whether the English word "body" is the most appropriate one. In Sanskrit, the words used to signify these two bodies of the Buddha are dharmakāya and rūpakāya. The first is of the nature of mind, whereas the latter is material. So when the Buddha passes away, there is still this more subtle body, which is of the nature of mind, and since the mental continuum is also present, we can say that the personality is still there. Even today, the Buddha remains as a living being. I think this is better, don't you? I don't think it a very pleasing proposition that living sentient beings at some point completely disappear.

Now, this third category of suffering is the body which acts as the basis of all other suffering. And as we mentioned, it is transcended in Nirvāṇa. This does not mean, however, that great beings cease to exist, but instead that their gross, impure physical form and limited consciousness comes to be replaced by the two types of pure bodies of an enlightened being.

Question: **Please explain the benefits of becoming ordained as opposed to practicing the Dharma as a lay person.**

His Holiness: In the Vinaya Sūtra, it is explained that there are many different levels of ordination. Even taking the five *upāsaka* vows is considered lay ordination. Then, of course, there is the ordination of monks and nuns. Even though we may be engaged upon a similar course of virtuous action before and after taking ordination, nonetheless, when we take certain vows and keep them, there is a great difference in the benefits. After taking vows, not only are we engaged in virtue, but due to having made a promise, to having taken a pledge in a positive direction, it represents a further or more extended commitment on our part. To take ordination means to take vows, to promise something, and to create a certain determination. So of course it is bound to make a difference.

Now, as regards the differences between lay ordination and that of monks and nuns, since the latter two take the vow of celibacy, it means that they do not have families. Ultimately, what this means is that monks and nuns have more freedom. If one is married, any major decision cannot be made alone, but only in consultation with one's spouse. Monks and nuns, however, have more independence and of course have more time to pursue spiritual practice. Also, though the desire for the opposite sex may not be extinguished completely, by having taken ordination, there is a certain checking or mindfulness present that is very helpful. This makes a difference. Also, in terms of belongings, a *bhikṣu*, or fully ordained monk, for example, is allowed to possess only thirteen kinds of articles. These are the only things he can consider his own. Anything additional is allowed to be kept only with the understanding that "this belongs to myself as well as someone else." So, though in practice I may use something that is not among the thirteen articles, and though in practice it may for all intents and purposes be mine, I must always keep the mental attitude that it is a shared thing. The three robes (which must always be kept with one) and these thirteen articles are, according to the Vinaya Sūtra, a monk's sole possessions. This is of course very helpful in checking our desire, in controlling and weakening attachment. This is one of the benefits of being an ordained monk or nun. In both the Sūtrayāna and the Tantric scriptures, the Buddha himself has mentioned that the benefits of a single virtuous action will vary according to the basis, i.e. according to whom it is that performs it. It is for these reasons that the Buddha himself, the son of a king, sacrificed his entire kingdom to become a monk. He practiced austerities for six years and then, under the Bodhi tree, he became enlightened. All of these actions he did in order to show his followers the right path to achieve Buddhahood. This does not mean, however, that in order to achieve Buddhahood one must become a monk or nun. This is not the case. Without becoming a monk or nun, it is possible to achieve full enlightenment.

Question: **How do the ideas about emptiness differ in the different schools of Tibetan Buddhism?**

His Holiness: Tibetan Buddhism, as you know, contains the teachings of the Hīnayāna, of the ordinary Mahāyāna, or Sūtrayāna, and of the special Mahāyāna, or the secret teachings of the Tantra. So Tibetan Buddhism is a complete form of Buddhism. Now, the Tibetan tradition, from a historical viewpoint, is divided into the Old School (*rNying ma*) and the New Schools (*gSar ma*). The latter, in turn, is generally said to include the Kagyu, Sakya, and Kadam traditions. The last of these later became the Gelug tradition. So in general there are four schools, one Old School and three New Schools, though of course within these there are many subdivisions.

All of these four sects teach a combination of Sūtrayāna and Mantrayāna doctrines. Within the Mantrayāna, they especially teach the Tantras of the Anuttarayoga class, in combination again with the ordinary Mahāyāna doctrines of the Sūtrayāna. There are many words used to designate emptiness (*stong pa nyid*) in Tibetan. There is the word *nay lug* (*gnas lugs*, lit. "the way things are"), as well as *day ko na nyi* (*de kho na nyid*, lit. "thusness" or "reality"). According to the Sūtrayāna, this refers for the most part to emptiness as an object. In the Anuttarayoga Tantra system, however, the word *nay lug* refers primarily to the subject side, to the *experience* of emptiness, to the special consciousness which understands reality in the Tantric system, namely the clear light. Actually, clear light can refer to two things, an object or a subject. The former kind of clear light is the object emptiness. The latter is the consciousness which possesses this emptiness as its object, the clear light proper. But the phrase "clear light" is used to refer to both of these aspects. So it corresponds to the words "emptiness" and "the way things are" in the Sūtrayāna.

Now in terms of the actual practice, when one is immersed in the contemplation of the clear light, since all dualistic appearances vanish, it becomes impossible to distinguish the object from the consciousness perceiving it. They seem to become as if they were one, like water mixed with water. Of course, strictly speaking, there are two entities, subject and object, but within the experience of the clear light this duality is lost.

In the Nyingma practice of Dzogchen (The Great Perfection) there are two entities called *tegchö* and *togel*. Tegchö refers to the practice and contemplation of the ultimate reality, it is the method for achieving the dharmakāya, whereas the togel is the method for achieving the rūpakāya. So we see that the clear light practice mentioned above is related to the tegchö practices of the Nyingma Dzogchen tradition. Also there are mentioned in the Dzogchen two other concepts: the nature (*ngo bo*), *kadag* (utter purity), and the essence (*rang bzhin*), *lhundub* (spontaneity). *Kadag* refers to emptiness, while *lhundub* refers to the subjective side of the clear light. It is the basis of both saṃsāra and of Buddhahood.

In the Kagyu tradition, we have, related to this topic, the Chagya Chenpo (The Great Seal). And in the Sakya school, we have concepts such as the Khorde Yermey (Indivisibility of Saṃsāra and Nirvāṇa) and Seltong Zungjug (The Union of Clarity and Emptiness) which are also related to that topic. In the Gelug tradition there is Deytong Yermey (The Indivisibility of Bliss and Emptiness), and especially the type of Deytong Yermey called Lhenkyey Kyi Deytong Yermey (The Indivisibility of Spontaneous Bliss and Emptiness) is what is analogous to the above. So, from this viewpoint, all four Tibetan sects ultimately come together on this point.

There is, however, one school of thought called Zhentong (The Emptiness of All Others), which seems to depart from the above interpretations of emptiness. But according to Khyentse Rinpoche, there are two kinds of Zhentong; one is acceptable, the other is not quite correct. Many Tibetan Buddhist scholars in ancient times very seriously refuted that latter type of Zhentong. In this interpretation of emptiness, the absolute was viewed as being empty of all conventional phenomena, and the absolute truth itself became absolute, and not a mere conventionally existing entity. This viewpoint is incorrect. It contradicts Nāgārjuna's teachings and it contradicts what is taught in the Buddha's second turning of the wheel, the *Prajñāpāramitā Sūtras*. Nāgārjuna himself said that no phenomenon exists absolutely, and this applies even to emptiness itself. Even the absolute truth does not exist absolutely. He said that every phenomenon depends on other factors, that they arise interdependently. That is why every phenomenon is of the nature of emptiness, and the absolute, emptiness itself, is no exception. The Buddha himself made this quite clear in teaching the sixteen, eighteen, or twenty different kinds of emptiness, for in these lists he included "the emptiness of emptiness" (*stong pa nyid stong pa nyid*), and "the emptiness of the absolute" (*don dam pa stong pa nyid*).

Question: **For a person who is rooted in the practice of vipaśyanā, is there a particular Tibetan Buddhist practice that you feel would be complementary?**

His Holiness: I would like to know what you mean by the word "vipaśyanā."

Questioner: **I mean insight meditation the way it is practiced in the Theravada tradition.**

His Holiness: Yes, but what kind of Theravada vipaśyanā are you referring to?

Questioner: **To the practice of watching the breath, watching the body, the feelings etc.**

His Holiness: Then within this you do not include the practice of selflessness, of *anatman*?

Questioner: **Perhaps it is not specifically included, but it comes as a result.**

His Holiness: When you concentrate on the breathing, try shifting your attention to the thought which is concentrating on the breathing. This may serve to complement your practice. While you are concentrated on the breath, try to analyze or investigate the nature of the thought or mind which is aware of the breathing. Try to notice the kind of thoughts that come. Eventually, you will become acquainted with the nature of the thought. Then try to stop the memory of past things, and try to bring a halt to thinking about the future. Without thoughts of the past and future, merely remaining in the present, try to avoid any particular thought. Try to see what happens then, what you experience. Sometimes this is called thoughtlessness. It is coming to an understanding of thought, then relaxing in such a way that the activity of thought becomes reduced. I think that might be a complement to your daily practice. Do you practice anything like this?

Questioner: **Well, as part of vipaśyanā instruction we are told to be mindful of our thoughts as well. But I was wondering whether there was anything by way of mantra repetition that might enhance one's practice of vipaśyanā?**

His Holiness: I think the Manjuśrī mantra *Oṃ Arapacana Dhiḥ*, or simply *Dhiḥ*, would be helpful. Just reciting *Dhiḥ* repeatedly, one single syllable, may be enough. Then try to investigate "to whom does this thought belong?," "who am I?" If you do this properly, you will find that there is no independent "I," you will find an absence, or emptiness, of such a self. Still, there is some sort of a self, there is an "I," there is an American. Are you American?

Questioner: **Yes.**

His Holiness: So there will still be an American, but he just won't be able to be found. This kind of investigation is useful.

Question: **Your Holiness mentioned that we should meditate on the nature of mind. Could you give some instructions as to how this is to be done.**

His Holiness: Half of the question I have just answered above. It is necessary to investigate or analyze thought. And especially when you become angry or when strong desire arises, forget about the object toward which you feel anger or desire, and instead investigate the nature of the anger or desire itself. Sometimes when you feel very tired and you lay prostrate almost unable to move, it seems that at such times some persons may be able to experience a somewhat deeper level of consciousness. Likewise, during a serious illness, when one's body, one's physical part, becomes very weak, almost to the point of dying, then deeper and more subtle levels of consciousness become more active. At this time, some people undergo some extraordinary experiences. Such times are excellent opportunities for analyzing the nature of consciousness, or rather of the deeper levels of consciousness. Some people, close to death, experience certain kinds of inner appearances, whitish, reddish, darkness, etc. This seems to happen. So this is a good opportunity to investigate.

Question: **We heard that next year Your Holiness will be giving the Kālacakra initiation in Bodhgaya. What are the prerequisites to attend it, and what is the special significance of receiving this initiation?**

His Holiness: As usual, in order to properly receive the Kālacakra initiation, it is necessary to have at least some experience of *bodhicitta,* or altruism, and some understanding of emptiness, or clear light. At this point, I sometimes contradict myself. The other day one of my friends asked me this very question. He said that since the Kālacakra is one of the highest teachings of the Tantrayāna, it may not be very useful to receive it without the proper preparation and prerequisites. First he asked me whether for any of the higher tantric practices these prerequisites were necessary, and I said "yes." Then his next question was about Kālacakra, and here is where I contradicted myself. You see, with the Kālacakra, there are not many restrictions. I myself do not know the reason for this. For entering the other maṇḍalas such as that of Guhyasamāja, Heruka, or Hevajra, etc., there are many restrictions and it is meant to be a very limited affair. Especially in the Sakya tradition, the latter initiation can be given only to twenty-five among them. So, for example, if there are one hundred persons, the initiation must be repeated four times. I think this is a very good tradition. But with Kālacakra, there is no restriction. As I have explained before, I feel that the Kālacakra maṇḍala is somehow associated with the kingdom, with the community, with society. Also, although no one knows where Śambhala is, it nonetheless does seem to exist. Though ordinary people cannot see it or communicate with it at this moment through ordinary means, after some time it may become clear how to do this. According to the scriptures, Śambhala will eventually make contact with our own world. In brief, the maṇḍala of Kālacakra is not like other maṇḍalas. Other Tantric practices are related to the individual, but the Kālacakra seems to be related to the community, to the global society as a whole. Perhaps this is the reason why the restrictions are eased when a lama gives the Kālacakra initiation. The benefit, therefore, is this, namely, that even though the disciple may not be prepared fully, somehow a connection is created through having obtained the initiation, so that later when Śambhala interacts with the world community, there will perhaps be some positive effect. But I myself am not very clear on this point, it is only my opinion.

Question: **Could Your Holiness explain something about protectors in Tibetan Buddhism. I am confused on whether to regard them as sentient beings, as symbols, or as part of my own and others' consciousnesses. If they are local gods and deities of Tibet that have been subdued, as I have heard some say, how can they have universal effect or benefit?**

His Holiness: I agree, this is a source of confusion. Among the Tibetans there is too much emphasis on protectors. As a Buddhist, the real protector is oneself. Since we believe in karma, that what we reap is a result of our own action, the real protection is our own good action, a good mind, a good motivation. This is the real protector.

The system of protectors actually comes from the Tantrayāna. Since protectors are connected with the Tantras, to engage in the practices related to these protectors it is necessary for the adept to first gain some experience of mental visualization. Once one has a certain amount of experience of deity yoga, then, based on that, one can imagine protectors and give them work to do, either the work of pacifying, or of increasing (long-life or wealth, etc.), of power, or wrathful work. So, based on one's own practice of deity yoga, one gives them instructions on what they must do.

Now there are many different kinds of protectors. Consider, for example, the ten wrathful kings (*mahākrodharāja*). They are protectors. They are the manifestations of the Buddha's ten limbs. Or again, in the *Abhidharmakośa*, ten different kinds of minds are described. Hence, these ten protectors can be considered manifestations of the Buddha's ten kinds of mind. Because these are manifestations of an enlightened being, they must be considered to be supramundane, beyond saṃsāra.

Then there is another category of protector, such as Vaiśravaṇa (rNam thos sras), who are not the manifestation of a buddha, but instead, of a bodhisattva. So this is a category of protector which is mundane and still within saṃsāra. Now, within this latter category there are some protectors, like the Five-Bodied King (rGyal po sku lnga) who, though in saṃsāra, are not exclusively Tibetan protectors, since they operate in much wider realms, in a much larger world. And yet, there is another kind of worldly protector who is associated with a particular place or people. I, for example, come from a region of Tibet known as Amdo. There, our local protector is Machen Bomra. This is a deity whose activities are very localized within this particular area.

In some cases, these deities influence events within the world. There are even some instances in which they have appeared in Chinese prisons after the Chinese takeover. It's actually quite mysterious. Here is one strange story. Very recently, one Tibetan who comes from the Amdo area went back to visit her native place. While there, she had a vision of the local deity and they conversed. During their conversation, the deity told her that he had gone to China to prison, and that after that he had spent eleven years in India with me. Nobody, however, gave these statements in and of themselves very much credence.

But then the story continues. In this area, you see, it was the custom for the local people to offer tsampa (roasted barley flour) and milk to the deity. In addition, they offered roasted meat. This was the tradition in this area. It seems, however, that the protector mentioned that while he was around the Dalai Lama, he received some teachings, and that since then, he prefers to refrain from taking meat. He told the local people who propitiate him that on this one occasion, since they had already gone to the trouble of preparing the meat, he would accept it. He made it quite clear, though, that in the future they should no longer offer him meat.

Now I have given the Kālacakra initiation in Bodhgaya, Ladakh, Lahoul-Spiti, Arunachal Pradesh, etc. On these occasions, I visualize the different protectors of the Tibetan people, of Tibet as a community. I visualize that they are present there. I also instruct those who come from areas like Ladakh and Arunachal Pradesh that if they are performing animal sacrifices to propitiate the local deities, they should stop. I explain that it is wrong, that it is not the Buddhist way to make such offerings. I think this kind of advice may have had some effect on the protectors present there. So there may indeed be some connection between this and the reports of this one deity refusing meat.

These protectors, or deities, are mundane. They are within saṃsāra. They are also located at or associated with a particular place. These particular protectors have no specific connection to the West. Trungpa Rinpoche told me, however, that around his place there are many American protectors, American deities. However, let me say that, as a Buddhist, one should not be overly concerned with these protectors — it is not something of great priority. What should be important in our lives are the three jewels, the Buddha, Dharma, and Saṅgha. They are our ultimate protectors, our ultimate aim, and our ultimate friend. There is no need for a protector over and above these. So why complicate things for ourselves?

Question: **Recently, it has become quite easy for foreigners to visit Tibet. Does Your Holiness feel that there is any useful purpose in Western Dharma practitioners spending time in Tibet these days?**

His Holiness: I think that this is very worthwhile. First of all, it would give you the opportunity to see what Tibet is like. You can get first-hand experience of the country. Since you have some awareness of the Tibetan situation and of our traditions, to actually visit Tibet could be a very worthwhile and rewarding experience.

From a Tibetan viewpoint, someone who is practicing Tibetan Buddhism is considered a friend. So, were someone to visit that unfortunate place as a friend and express a feeling of warmth and solidarity for those unfortunate people, it would give them some inspiration and courage.

It used to be that the Chinese characterized the Tibetan situation by saying that Tibet was four things: too cruel, too backward, too dark, and too barbaric. Some time back, however, at a special function, they said that perhaps the word "too" was a bit extreme. So they modified their position. Now, they claimed, the situation in Tibet was "cruel," but not "too cruel," "dark," but not "too dark," etc.

It would be worthwhile for Western Buddhists to visit Tibet so as to demonstrate that Tibetan culture does have something to offer the world; that especially Tibetan Buddhism is something useful, not only for Tibetans, whom the Chinese consider "cruel," backwards," and "in darkness," but even for civilized Westerners, whom they used to regard as reactionary capitalists, but whom they now consider friends.

You see, the Chinese dislike your ideology, your economic system, and your politics. But because of your scientific and technological progress, they are very much looking toward the Western society as a model. So it will be a good lesson, it well be very helpful for them to see that someone from such a society has found something useful in Tibetan culture, in the practice of Tibetan Buddhism, for example.

Question: **What are the karmic circumstances that must be understood and purified if the problem of poverty, especially in the non-industrialized societies, is to be alleviated?**

His Holiness: Of course, as Buddhists, we believe that in any situation there is at play an external force and an internal one. Take the question of economic success, for example. Tibetans are refugees in India and in other countries throughout the world. Now, I am not implying that there are not several thousand Tibetans whose living conditions are very poor — who undergo great difficulties, and whom it is our responsibility to help. Overall, however, Tibetans have been quite successful. They have done quite well in the economic sphere.

In Tibet itself there were many families who, because they were classified as belonging to the "upper class," were tormented, physically beaten, and had their property seized. But despite the fact that their wealth was taken from them, somehow they were still quite successful. If they had just a few cows left, these animals managed to provide them with more or better milk. Whatever the causes, they managed to do quite well for themselves despite persecution. On the other hand, some poor families, despite the fact that they were given heavy subsidies by the Chinese, have remained poor. This implies that there seem to be other factors, inner factors, at work.

It is our custom to say that someone is "lucky" or "unlucky" if they meet with fortunate or unfortunate circumstances, respectively. It is however too simplistic to think in terms of random "luck." Even from a scientific point of view, this is not a sufficient explanation. Should something unfortunate happen, we immediately think, "Oh, how unlucky!" And yet, this is not sufficient to explain what happened — there must be a cause. Likewise, when we think that successful people are very lucky, we are overlooking the fact that that too has a cause. We seem to call "luck" that factor which overrides external conditions to bring about a positive situation. But that too is a cause; it is an inner cause, which we call "merit."

Changing weather patterns and natural disasters, for example, are definitely related to the karmic force of the local people involved. There are four external elements: earth, fire, water (or liquid), and air (or energy). There are also four internal elements which are related to anger, desire, and ignorance. Though there is no *direct* connection, still, indirectly the behavior of the individual is somehow connected to the change of the environment or external conditions. To put it briefly, then, any set of circumstances is characterized by two sets of factors, external and internal. To change a given situation, both external *and* internal changes must take place.

Question: **During your last trip to the United States, you had some contact with the American Indians, and you also participated in an American Indian fire ceremony. I was wondering if you see any karmic connection between the Indians and their plight and the Tibetans and their plight.**

His Holiness: Actually, I never participated in a fire ceremony, but I do have some Indian friends. It is an interesting question. When comparing American Indians and Tibetans, I think that there are similarities, but also many differences. I think there are some differences between the white invaders that the Indians faced and the Chinese invaders we faced. From one viewpoint, it is not my business, not for me to say. And yet, I feel that the best thing for American Indians to do is, as many of them already do, to live peacefully and in friendship with white Americans, since the modern American nation itself is multi-racial, multi-cultural, and multi-religious. When the Chinese and the Russians criticize the American system, they may have some valid points. But whatever else may be the case, Americans enjoy full liberty. Americans on the whole are nice people. As in every human community, there are bad people, but on the whole, they are good people. So, from my viewpoint, it seems to me that the best policy the Indians could adopt is one of reconciliation, of learning to live together.

Now let us consider the Tibetan case. I mentioned the other day at the public teachings that there exists a certain pillar constructed by a Tibetan king about one thousand years ago which says that the Chinese are much happier in China, and the Tibetans are much happier in Tibet. Chinese are very fond of rice and seafood, which you can't get in Tibet. So it's much better for them to remain in China. We Tibetans prefer tsampa (roasted barley flour), which we cannot get in China. So naturally, we feel much more at home in Tibet.

Question: **Will Your Holiness give some advice on how to get a Buddhist center started in Bodhgaya that could benefit both Indian and Western people?**

His Holiness: The idea is a very good one, but I have no specific suggestions on how to achieve that goal. Of course, as in the case of every noble task, the motivation should be clear and sincere. This is most important. If this is present, then, despite setbacks, a sound and stable determination will carry one through.

This place is, for the Buddhist world, perhaps the most sacred place. But if I may say so, it is also one of the dirtiest places. It makes it difficult to visit, which is unfortunate. Because this site is so important, I opt for coming every year. But before coming, I resign myself to sacrificing my nose. By visiting Bodhgaya, it is almost guaranteed that I will come down with the flu. Yet what this goes to prove is that Bodhgaya is a very active and important place.